In sea
Sec...
Norfolk

A Souvenir and Guide to Norfolk

Robert Leader

THOROGOOD

Published by Thorogood

10-12 Rivington Street

London EC2A 3DU

Telephone: 020 7749 4748

Fax: 020 7729 6110

Email: info@thorogood.ws

Web: www.thorogood.ws

A CIP catalogue record for this book is available from the British Library.

ISBN 1 85418 372 9

Printed in India by Replika Press

Designed by Driftdesign

CONTENTS

ILLUSTRATIONS

INTRODUCTION

Norfolk is a unique county, there is no other in England which is quite like it. The bulging coastline begins at the mouth of The Wash, where King John lost his treasure. It continues in a fascinating curve of creeks and marshes, cliffs and sand dunes, until it reaches the splendid golden beaches of fun-filled, bustling Great Yarmouth, the seaside capital of East Anglia. This grand eastward sweep includes charming little fishing villages and genteel Edwardian towns, the wide-sky lonely places haunted only by wheeling seagulls, walkers and bird-watchers, and the great port centres of maritime heritage and history. In the sea breeze and the salt air you can still taste the memory of the herring fishing, the golden age when there was still the silver harvest to be reaped.

The interior of the county is an equally diverse mixture, the bracken and bramble filled forests of Breckland, where wild deer and rabbits still roam; the misty and mysterious Fenlands; the water-maze, reed-fringed wonderland of the Broads, the holiday playground of a multitude of sailing boats and motor cruisers. At the heart of it all lies Norwich, a mediaeval and modern university city, which somehow manages to blend the best of all possible worlds.

In Search Of Secret Norfolk charts the heritage and history through chapters on its great Norman castles and Abbeys, on the guildhalls and wool churches that grew up with mediaeval trade, and the stately homes of the great land-owning families who helped to shape it all. Other chapters follow the rivers, wandering the Wensum, the blue highway of the Bure, and the Yare which flows from the city to the sea. The Great Ouse winds through Fenland. The Thet forms part of the Norfolk/Suffolk border. Together they all help build up a comprehensive picture of the county as a whole.

Secret Norfolk features over 100 illustrations and follows the successful format of *In Search of Secret Suffolk,* also written and photographed by Robert Leader. The book is designed as the ideal companion for the resident of the county, and the perfect guide and souvenir for the visitor.

Norfolk's castles –
A history in stone

1

1 NORFOLK'S CASTLES – A HISTORY IN STONE

Castles are romantic places. Those ruined stone walls, where we find them today, are wreathed in the colourful imagery of myth and history. Stand on any crumbling battlement and imagination runs riot with scenes of attack and defence, siege and splendour. Jousting champions charge again, with visors down and pennants streaming from their lances. Graceful ladies dance in their gorgeous mediaeval costumes, jesters tumble and minstrels delicately pluck their lutes to the tune of *Greensleeves*.

CASTLE ACRE,
THE REMAINS OF
THE WEST GATE

THE GATEWAY INTO CASTLE RISING

During the Middle Ages the Normans built over 1500 castles around the British Isles, and Norfolk has its fair share of some of their still proud remains. Castle Acre and Castle Rising are two of the best known sites, and here on a good day you can still see re-enactments of those glory days, when the great halls were alive with feasting and merriment, or the walls under siege to the clash of swords and axes.

Perhaps the oldest remaining castle site in Norfolk is Burgh Castle, a few miles south-west of Great Yarmouth. The Normans built upon Burgh Castle but the original walls pre-date 1066, and were in fact built long before Great Yarmouth. The Romans built Burgh as one of a great chain of forts designed to keep out the Saxon sea raiders during the later years of their declining empire.

Now the old walls look out over peaceful Breydon Water, where on balmy days the white sails of pleasure boats drift by in the sunshine, but in those days long past, Breydon Water was a large open estuary to the sea. It was an easy inland route for the attacking pirates and a fleet of Roman war galleys would have been stationed here to stop them.

The long walls stand some seventeen feet high, ten feet wide at the base but narrowing toward the top, and they now enclose a huge grassy open space of about six acres. They are constructed of flint with layers of flat brick, like layers of brown icing in crumbling black cake. The Normans added a great mound and a keep to turn the fort into a castle, but those have long since gone. Now only the original walls remain, a two thousand year old testament to the construction skills of their Roman builders.

Castle Acre was built soon after the Norman Conquest. All those French knights and adventurers who had gambled their lives at the Battle of Hastings were now reaping their rewards. William the Conqueror had taken the Crown of England and was busy dividing up his new lands among his friends and allies. Castle Acre was among the Norfolk estates given by the new King to William of Warrene, who later became Chief Justiciar and the first of the powerful Earls of Surrey, who continued to play important roles in their new nation's affairs.

The castle was built where the ancient route of the Peddars Way crossed the River Nar, a busy crossroads for horse and river traffic at the time, and England's kings were quite frequent visitors here en route to the great pilgrimage shrine at Walsingham. It comprised a massive earth mound on two levels, encircled by a great moat ditch. It was originally defended by a wooden palisade but this was later replaced by two stone curtain walls. The lower level contained the Great Hall, kitchens, storehouses, stables and workshops, servants' quarters and space to crowd in the surrounding villagers in the event of an attack.

CASTLE ACRE, LOOKING FROM THE CURTAIN WALL TO THE REMAINS OF THE KEEP

The upper level was the residence of the Castle Lord and the nobility, and was initially a large country house. This was later developed into a massive stone walled keep after the Conqueror died and his sons and their descendants plunged England into a period of civil wars as contenders for the throne. The keep would also have been the last place of resort in a siege, but despite the troubled times it was fortunately never put to the test.

Today the castle site is a large picnic area between the ruins of the old curtain walls. The lower part of the keep is all that remains of its once crowning glory, almost swallowed up in the surrounding earth bank of the higher level. The crumbling west gateway once connected the castle to the small town of Castle Acre, which was also fortified, and there is a handsome stone Bailey Gate still standing in the town.

However, if you want to build up the full picture, pay a visit to Castle Rising where the magnificent keep still stands to its full height in almost all its original glory. Old records and reconstruction drawings show that the keep at Castle Acre would have looked very much like its splendid surviving cousin at Castle Rising.

It is possible that this site also boasted some earlier Roman fortifications as it was once a small port on the River Babingley. This access to the sea has long since silted up, and now the nearest port on The Wash is King's Lynn some five miles to the southwest. However, when William de Albini began the construction of Castle Rising around 1138 it was probably to protect the old port on the tidal estuary.

The whole site covered up to twelve acres with a gigantic earthwork topped by a stone curtain wall that had a circumference of around one thousand feet. The walls of the great tower keep still rise fifty feet high and only the original roof is missing. Its sheer size makes it an impressive sight even now, and with its huge stone staircase leading up through the ornate forebuilding on its east face it must have been magnificent in its day.

Like Castle Acre, Castle Rising was fortunate in that it was never called upon to face a siege. Norwich Castle, which was founded by the Conqueror himself was not so lucky. It was besieged for three months in 1075 when the then Earl of Norfolk rebelled against the King. William had given the Earldom, the City of

Norwich, and the castle to Ralph Guader, but almost immediately Ralph turned against him. William had briefly returned to Normandy and Ralph was soon plotting a conspiracy behind his back.

THE SPLENDID
KEEP AT
CASTLE RISING

However, one of Ralph's co-conspirators betrayed him in turn to the Archbishop of Canterbury, whom William had left in charge of his English kingdom during his absence. A loyal army was raised and led by two Bishops and Ralph was forced to flee to Denmark.

Ralph was soon back with a fleet of 200 Danish ships to support his rebellion. By then King William had quickly returned from France and, faced with the King's army, Ralph fled once more and his Danish allies fled with him. The old Viking appetite for rape and plunder was perhaps never quite so keen for a real fight. Ralph left his wife to hold Norwich Castle, but after the three month siege she surrendered.

Later control of the castle seems to have passed to and fro between the reigning King and the rebellious Bigod family who were forever scheming and siding with one power bloc or another. William was either a bad judge of his friends, or there were too few honest ones in his ranks, for Roger Bigod whom he next promoted as his Bailiff and Constable of Norwich Castle, proved along with his descendents to be as unreliable as Earl Ralph.

Henry I built the magnificent stone keep during the 1120s, but when King Henry II faced a rebellion from his own son, another Prince Henry, another Bigod, Hugh Bigod, was reigning in Norwich Castle. Hugh Bigod was soon at the heart of this new rebellion, siding with the Prince against the King. Hugh raised a Flemish army and brought it across the North Sea to England. He expected Norwich to support him but when the city stayed loyal to the crown he attacked and burned it down. The King's army again marched into East Anglia and Hugh surrendered.

A generation later history repeated itself yet again. The Bigods had bought back their castles and their titles from King Richard the Lionheart, who needed money to finance his crusades to the Holy Lands. His brother John now sat on the Throne of

England and was involved in another bitter civil war with his Barons. Another Roger Bigod ruled in Norwich Castle and pitted his strength against his King.

This time there was something useful in the outcome. Roger Bigod was one of those Barons who swore the oath which ultimately forced John to sign the Magna Carta, the Great Charter which became the foundation of English government and law.

After all the plots and counter plots of the Middle Ages, England, Norfolk and Norwich slowly became more stable. As the turbulent succession of Bigods ceased to stalk its walls, the castle's role in Norwich history seems to have become mainly one of witnessing executions. The castle finally became the city goal, and a long list of villains and heroes were hanged, and sometimes even drawn and quartered at the end of the Castle Bridge.

Norwich was frequently a centre for riots and discontent over food prices and shortages, mayoral elections, or land enclosures and property disputes. One major outbreak was Kett's Rebellion in 1549. It led to a government army of over 13,000, led by the Earl of Warwick, being sent to restore order after a full-scale battle with the rebels, and Robert Kett, the rebel leader, being hanged from the top of Norwich Castle.

In 1648 another riot ended with a huge explosion when a gunpowder store was ignited and 40 people were reported killed. Of the 66 people charged with being involved in the rioting eight of them were subsequently hanged in the castle ditches, along with two unfortunate old women who had received their death sentence on separate charges of witchcraft.

The public hangings outside the castle continued until the middle of the 19th century and up to 30,000 spectators could be drawn to watch such an event. Now Norwich Castle serves only as the city museum and recently the superb, fully restored keep has been given another major facelift. However, a few grim death masks of those who gruesomely died to entertain an earlier public still remain on display inside.

For the enthusiastic castle hunter there are other sites in Norfolk that should not be neglected. At Thetford there is the huge motte mound which is all that remains of another castle that was once held by the notorious Hugh Bigod, until it was confiscated and destroyed by Henry II in 1157.

The Thetford mound, at 80 feet, is the tallest mediaeval earthwork in Britain. In two great loops at its base are more grassed-over earthworks that were once defensive banks and ditches. 1500 years before the Normans an Iron Age fort stood here, dominating the land and river crossroads where the rivers Thet and Ouse intermingled.

At Weeting, Baconsthorpe and Old Buckenham there are more castle ruins.

The three-foot thick, three storey high walls at Weeting are the crumbling remnants of a 12th century castle that once covered some four hundred square feet. At Baconsthorpe there are ruined walls and a corner gatehouse dating back to the 15th century. At New Buckenham there are ancient earthworks and the lower level of a circular keep, and at Mileham there is a motte and the stump remains of yet another tower keep.

There are traces of other long gone castles from those turbulent middle ages scattered around Norfolk, most of them just earth mounds to show where they once stood. However, the one remaining castle of note is Caister Castle, one of the earliest major buildings in England to be constructed of brick instead of the usual flint and rubble.

THE DOMINANT
TOWER OF
CAISTER CASTLE

Caister Castle was built in the early 15th century, much later than the great Norman keeps, and owes its design more to continental influences. By now the invention of gunpowder and canon had marked the beginning of the end of the great age

of mediaeval castles, but Caister Castle was still a strongly fortified home. It was built by Sir John Fastolfe, said to be the
inspiration for Shakespeare's Falstaff. However, it seems that
Shakespeare made a cruel caricature of the man by totally
reversing his character as Fastolf is said to have been a bril-
liant soldier who fought with distinction at Agincourt, at the
siege of Rouen and the capture of Caen.

After his military career was over he sited his castle home close
to the River Bure as a defence against a possible Flemish invasion.
The feared invasion never came but in 1458 the castle garrison
did fight off a gang of marauding pirates.

After Sir John's death the ownership of the castle fell into dispute.
In 1469 it fell to a five week siege by the Duke of Norfolk who
surrounded it with three thousand men. It was an almost blood-
less victory with the defenders beaten by lack of food and
gunpowder, and perhaps the mediaeval equivalent of sending
in the bailiffs.

Today its great north-west tower, five storeys high, still rises
triumphant above the remaining walls, reflected in the calm
waters of the moat. The castle ruins are a tourist attraction and
there is a purpose built museum holding a fascinating collection of old motor vehicles and related exhibits.

Visit any castle site and you will find a part of the history of
Norfolk, and indeed of all England, written in the silent,
haunted stones. They stood against foreign invasion, and they
and their rulers played their roles in all the political and power
intrigues of the realm. Their golden age has gone, consigned
to history, but the tales they have to tell will live as long as the
eroding stones remain.

Norfolk's abbeys – the ecclisiastical glory of the Middle Ages

2

2 NORFOLK'S ABBEYS – THE ECCLISIASTICAL GLORY OF THE MIDDLE AGES

In mediaeval England the church was a power to equal the King. Perhaps it was even more than equal, for the King was a remote figure, never seen by the vast majority of his subjects, while the church was a routine part of their weekly lives. Few people in those days ever questioned the validity of the Catholic faith, and almost every peasant flocked to mass on Sundays.

Early monastic communities were founded to enable groups of monks or nuns to live apart from the general population, but after the Conquest the new Norman Lords and Barons vied with each other to found new Abbeys, Monasteries and Priories. A great and glorious age of monolithic church building had begun and lasted until the reign of Henry VIII and the Dissolution, and in Norfolk many of their most splendid ruins still remain.

At Castle Acre, Thetford, Binham and Creak there are still magnificent reminders of those mediaeval days of ecclesiastical glory, scattered in jewels of wind-scoured flint and rain-bleached stone that still defy the efforts of time, and man, and the elements to obliterate them entirely.

The ruins of the great Cluniac Priory at Castle Acre, together with the ruins of the castle, both founded by William de Warrene, make this strategic little village on the junction of the River Nar and the ancient Peddars Way into one of the most fascinating historical sites in the county. Warrene, who became the First Earl of Surrey, had at some time visited the great Burgundian Abbey at Cluny and had become a member of that noble order. Like most of the French nobles who had triumphed with their swords in the vanguard with William the Conqueror, de Warrene immediately set work to defend his new English estates with a castle, but his piety also ensured the construction of the adjoining priory.

CASTLE ACRE, THE
SOUTH WEST
TOWER OF THE
PRIORY CHURCH

The great age of European monasticism was generally organized and revitalized by the Benedictines, the followers of Saint Benedict of Nursia. The first twelve Benedictine monasteries were founded in Italy early in the 6th century. The Clunaic order was a reformed Benedictine movement, which was noted for its strict adherence to the good Saint's founding rules.

The priory at Castle Acre consisted of a huge church, a chapter house and refectory, all built around the one-hundred foot square central cloister. Much of the elaborate decoration typical of the Cluniac style is still visible in the fine stonework that remains. Most of the west front and the south-west tower is still standing, together with the Prior's house built into the west face of the cloister.

The community was founded with 36 monks, and their waking hours would have been divided between the prayers and rituals celebrating the Divine Office, agricultural work, religious reading and study. The income needed to fund the priory came from de Warrene's landed estates, and from the income of the churches given to the community. The priory also enjoyed royal support from both Henry I and Henry II, although this also meant bearing the cost of housing the occasional royal visitors.

Norfolk's second great Cluniac priory was established at Thetford in 1103 by the notorious Roger Bigod, allegedly for the atonement of his manifold sins, and probably because it was much easier than making the long and dangerous pilgrimage to Jerusalem, which in those days was seen as the only alternative for a nobleman to achieve salvation.

It was originally settled with twelve monks in the centre of Thetford, but after a few years the community had grown and the priory was moved to a sprawling riverside site on the north bank of the Little Ouse, just above the junction with the Thet. There are extensive ruins here in this beautiful setting. Jagged pinnacles and archways of broken flint rise above the remnants of the once proud church walls, and nearby is an almost perfectly preserved gatehouse dressed in flush flint-work. There was a much venerated statue of the Virgin enshrined here which apparently worked miracles through dreams, and so made the priory an important place of pilgrimage.

Thetford in the Middle Ages had up to twelve religious houses, and on the other side of the river stand the remains of the smaller Priory of the Holy Sepulchre. Built to provide for the needs of pilgrims on their way to Jerusalem, it was founded by the third Earl of Surrey who died on the Second Crusade to the Holy Land.

THE REMAINS OF THE GREAT CLUNIAC PRIORY FOUNDED BY ROGER BIGOD AT THETFORD

The Priory of the Holy Sepulchre followed the rules of Saint Augustine of Hippo. The Augustinian friars kept to strict rules of poverty and saw their mission as one of preaching and tending the sick. They were one of a new wave of Holy Orders who took their faith to the people, rather than living in monastic isolation devoted mainly to the disciplines of prayer and ritual.

Another of their priories was founded by Robert Fitz Osbert near the ancient ferry crossing over the Waveny at St. Olaves. The priory here commemorated King Olaf, an 11th century King of Norway, who is said to have crusaded with the uncompromising message of "Baptism or death !"

Beeston Priory near Sheringham was also founded by the Augustinians in the 12th century. At all three sites only ruined walls remain.

Moving in toward central Norfolk, some twelve miles south-west of Norwich in the gentle green fields of the Tiffey valley, we find the massive twin towers of the great Abbey church at Wymondham. Founded in 1107 by William d'Albini, the church was intended to serve both Benedictine monks and the parishioners of Wymondham.

However, there was much quarreling between the two factions, especially over the ringing of the bells in the great octagonal central tower which was completed in 1409. The disputes were only solved some 30 years later when the parishioners built their own bell tower, the equally massive square West Tower. This division of interest no doubt saved the Abbey from falling into ruin after the Dissolution, for it was granted to the people of Wymondham after a payment of its valuation. Thus, this magnificent Abbey Church still survives intact to serve the people of Wymondham today.

Going back up towards the North Norfolk coast we find Binham Priory, a Benedictine Priory again founded in the late 11th century, this time by Pierre de Valoines, Lord of Oxford and a nephew of William the Conqueror. The parish church here was built on to the Norman nave after the reformation and is still in use, with the ruins of the priory adjoining. In 1222 the priory was besieged by forces rebelling against King John but was relieved by John's Chancellor, John de Grey, a loyal Norfolk man.

PINNACLES OF WIND-SCOURED FLINT ARE ALL THAT REMAIN OF BINHAM PRIORY

West of Binham are the ruins of Creake Abbey, another house of Augustinians which was much used by pilgrims on their way to the great pilgrimage site at Walsingham, which lies almost midway between Binham and Creake. One of Norfolk's most enigmatic treasure stories has its roots here. The monks are said to have buried a great hoard of gold and silver to keep it out of the greedy hands of King Henry VIII, but so far all attempt to find it have proved unsuccessful.

Two great abbeys once existed in the lonely marshes along the great rivers of the broads. St. Benet's Abbey stood on the north bank of the Bure, and Langley Abbey on the south bank of the Yare. St. Benet's was another Benedictine Abbey, and the only significant remains now are a 14th century gatehouse with the incongruous tower of an old windmill built inside. Langley was an Abbey of the Premonstratensian Order, founded in 1195. They were the White Canons, so-called because they wore white woollen cowls and robes. Langley was totally demolished at the Dissolution, its stones carried away for re-building elsewhere. Only its ghosts are said to remain to haunt the marshes.

Norwich is said to have had six orders of Friars in the Middle Ages, among them the Franciscans who were the Grey Friars, the Dominicans, the Black Friars, the Carmelite White Friars, and the Augustinian Friars, all with their separate houses in different parts of the city. However, the great Benedictine cathedral priory was always the heart of the city's religious life, and only the Cathedral survives.

So at last we come to Walsingham, England's Nazareth, and still a major centre for pilgrimage and worship. In 1061 the Lady of the Manor was at prayer when she beheld a vision of the Virgin Mary, who showed her the boyhood home of Jesus in Nazareth. The vision was repeated twice, until the good woman was convinced that she was being asked to build a replica of the Nazareth home on her own land in Norfolk. She obeyed the vision, and so Walsingham became the great focus of devotion and pilgrimage for all of those who could not make the long journey to the Holy Land.

In 1153 the Augustinian Canons came to Walsingham and built a huge priory to protect the shrine, and to attend to the religious needs of the multitudes of visitors. All that remains now is the great gateway, the ruined refectory and the magnificent east window. For 500 years Walsingham was a holy place, and the major centre of English religious experience. Then in the 1530s, like every other religious institution, it fell victim to the Reformation and the Dissolution.

The priory fell into ruins, but after another three centuries the Shrine of Our Lady at Walsingham was revived. There is now a beautiful new shrine, church and gardens, the restoration brought about by Father Hope Patten who was the Vicar of Walsingham from 1921 to 1958.

Streams of visitors and pilgrims flood into Walsingham throughout the summer months. Every Easter thousands come in groups, each group carrying its own cross to commemorate the last sad walk of Jesus. Walsingham is again the heart of faith and a flame of hope. The great buildings of religion may come and go, as all our majestic ruins testify throughout our county and our country, but faith and hope live on forever.

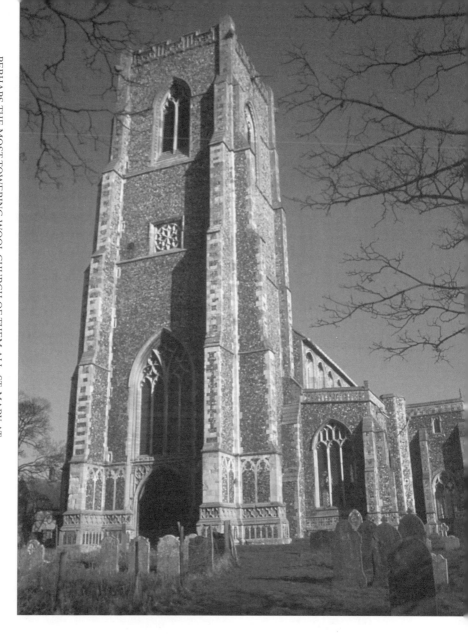

WOOL, THE WHITE GOLD OF NORFOLK

3

3 WOOL, THE WHITE GOLD OF NORFOLK

Thanks to its proximity to Europe, East Anglia in the Middle Ages was one of the most prosperous areas of Britain, and the rich legacy of those bygone times can still be seen today in the magnificent guildhalls, merchant's houses and wool churches that remain. In Suffolk and Essex the guildhalls and the homes of the rich merchants tended to be mainly timber and plaster Tudor constructions, but the good folk of Norfolk built most of theirs in magnificent flint-faced stone and brick.

NORFOLK'S WOOL WAS THE WHITE GOLD OF THE MIDDLE AGES

After the upheavals of the Norman Conquest the times were relatively peaceful, with much greater opportunities for trade with the continent. Much of the land that was reallocated from Saxons to Normans went to the large monastic foundations, and the churches and monastic orders proved generally good landowners who managed the land efficiently and filled their fields with sheep. The great Clunaic priory at Castle Acre was built with the profits from the new white gold that was Norfolk's wool. The market towns that became famous for their wool and cloth production flourished where there was easy transport and communication along the old Roman roads or rivers.

The guilds which grew in wealth and power with the wool trade were in effect the trade unions of the master craftsmen in an age before industrialization and the appearance of factories could concentrate all productivity under one roof. Individual weavers, spinners, dyers and the rest, all worked mostly in their own homes, and the guilds were the mediaeval way of forming themselves into brotherhoods to protect their own interests and the regulation of trade, wages, prices and standards.

There were guilds for other trades outside the scope of wool production, and church guilds which were foundations for social help and welfare formed around the churches. All guilds elected their own wardens and aldermen to act in the roles that would now be defined as chairman and committee members to debate and manage their affairs. The trade guilds also elected their own inspectors to guarantee that the quality of work and goods was maintained. There was always a strong sense of pride in ensuring the highest standards of craftsmanship.

However, the regulation of trade was not their only concern. There was no social security in those days, and so most craft guilds followed the church guilds in making some efforts to see to the welfare of any members and their families who might fall

on hard times through injury or old age. There were also ceremonial and religious events to be recognized and supported,
and each guild had its own dress and livery to be worn when
the occasion demanded. The guildsmen in their finery provided
a proud and colourful element in every important procession
that brought festive life and feasting to the prospering wool
towns.

NORWICH GUILDHALL

The two prime examples of Norfolk's guildhalls, those at Norwich
and King's Lynn, are both splendid brick buildings lavishly decorated and faced with cut black flint flushwork in elaborate design.
Both Norwich and Lynn were major ports in mediaeval times,
and both owed much of their prosperity to wool. In the early
centuries, immediately after the Norman Conquest, the exports
were mainly of the wool itself. Later, many of the wool towns,
and Norwich particularly, became thriving centres for the manufacture and export of thick worstead cloth.

The quality of Norfolk wool was best suited to the heavier cloth, and also the deep, fast-flowing rivers, though ideal for transport, were impractical for the finer techniques of washing and cleaning the lighter woollens. So Norwich and Norfolk concentrated on the worstead cloth, eventually gaining an almost complete monopoly.

This rapid growth was helped by a series of continental wars, floods and religious persecutions, which all helped to drive several waves of Flemish weavers to seek refuge in Norfolk. They were encouraged by an Act of 1337 in which King Edward III promised special privileges to all the cloth workers of other countries who would settle in England. During the reign of Elizabeth I there was another major influx of immigrants from the low counties, so that the mainly Flemish immigrants accounted for almost one third of the population of Norwich alone.

THE 15TH CENTURY GUILDHALL OF HOLY TRINITY AT KING'S LYNN

The Guildhall of the Holy Trinity overlooking the old Saturday Market Place in King's Lynn is a 15th century masterpiece of chequerboard flints, with a handsome three-storey porch and a huge arched window under a high gable, all of it fine enough to grace a cathedral. It was built between 1442 and 1448, replacing an earlier guildhall which had burned down.

In King's Street there also stands St. George's Guildhall, which now houses the Kings Lynn Arts Centre. Nowhere near as splendid externally as Holy Trinity, St. George's does have the distinction of being the oldest and the largest mediaeval guild-hall surviving in England. This huge, rectangular building was constructed between 1410 and 1420.

The Guildhall in Norwich is another prime example of Norfolk's ornate flint flushwork, and was the centre of the city's govern-ment from 1413 right down to the 20th century. It overlooks the huge multi-coloured square of canvas awnings that is the market place, beside the much larger City Hall that has now taken over it's old civic functions. Now it is the city's Information Centre.

Also overlooking the town market place, albeit a much smaller one, is the guildhall at Thetford, complete with an Edwardian clock tower and cupola. The original guildhall which stood here was also a mediaeval fantasy of black flint, but was almost entirely rebuilt at the turn of the 19th century. Like most of these ancient centres of commerce and local government it had a long and varied history, being part used as an armoury, council chambers, a courthouse and a workhouse. Perhaps its high spot was in entertaining Queen Elizabeth I in the summer of 1578 with a splendid ceremonial reception. The low was possibly the riots of 1792, which resulted in the mayor and his party being attacked by a mob of political rivals.

There was a guildhall at Blakeney, which was also once a thriving little port, but all that is left now is a vaulted brick undercroft where wool bales might once have been stored. East Dereham was once a major wool and cloth manufacturing centre with its own Guildhall of St. Withburga in the 15th century, but a more modern 18th century building stands on the original site and has now been incorporated into the modern Town Council offices.

IN EAST DEREHAM THESE ANCIENT COTTAGES AND THE SPLENDID CHURCH OF
ST. NICHOLAS ARE RICH REMINDERS OF ITS HERITAGE AS A WOOL TOWN

There were other major wool producing and cloth manufacturing centres in the Middle Ages at Attleborough, Aylsham, Diss, Harling and Horsham, Watton, Worstead and Wymondham. The wealth of the wool merchants in all these towns contributed greatly to the flowering of their great flint-towered churches from the 12th through to the 16th and 17th centuries, when the combination of weak kings, political taxes, foreign wars and the plague, accelerated the final decline of the wool trade.

Perhaps the most outstanding example is St. Mary's at Worstead, the village which gave its name to the well-known cloth. Built by the local weavers in 1379 the sheer size of the church and its dominating tower is out of all proportion to the small, scattered community which it serves.

Aylsham is a much larger market town where the wool and weaving industries flourished for over six centuries due to its fortunate position at the navigable head of the River Bure. The wool trade legacy here stands in the magnificent church of St. Michael and All Angels which overlooks the market square.

East Dereham is blessed with the beautiful parish church of St. Nicholas with its separate bell tower. The first church was founded here by St. Withburga in AD 654, although the present church has its origins in the 12th century. Much of the external structure is from the 13th century, with many later conversions and additions, including the massive south porch at the turn of the 16th century.

In all the great wool churches of North and West Norfolk, the continuing stages of furnishing, improving and extending the original structure were fuelled by wealth from the wool industry. All of it inspired by the faith and the pious hopes of the landowners, traders and merchants, who felt the need to praise and thank God for their incoming riches.

All of the old mediaeval guilds were dissolved in the late sixteenth century by the same Acts of Parliament that brought about the Dissolution of the Monasteries. The church guilds were an obvious target, and the trade guilds were included because of their own close associations with religion. In that age the entwined strands of faith, wealth and trade could not be separated.

The last stages of decline of the wool trade and its related industries soon followed, due to changing fashions and methods. The focus of trade shifted from the cold Baltic and the Rhineland to the warmer climate of the Mediterranean where thick Norwich worsteads and Norfolk woollens were no longer wanted. Lighter, brighter garments were the new fashion and production shifted to the North of England with the arrival of more modern machinery.

The mediaeval wool trade has gone but in some places the guildhalls themselves remain, and with them the splendid wool churches that still soar above the Norfolk market towns and village landscapes. They are part of Norfolk's glorious heritage, a permanent reminder of those mediaeval times when the fleece of the sheep was the white gold of Norfolk.

THE NORFOLK SHORE

4

4 THE NORFOLK SHORE

No shoreline ever stays the same. In prehistoric times it was ice ages and glaciers that carved the shape of our island and our shoulder of land that was once a peninsular bridge linking East Anglia with Europe. When the Romans came The Wash took a much wider and deeper bite than it does now, and there were deep sea creeks and estuaries all around the Norfolk coast. Since then the ceaseless pounding of the harsh North Sea has gnawed away the rough edges and silted up the seaways, to create the relatively rounded shape we see today.

The Roman sailor of two thousand years ago would simply not be able to find any of the harbours where once he moored his galleys. The coastal forts the legions built and manned have generally disappeared under the sea, along with several lost townships and villages, captured for ever by pounding gales, tidal surges and eroding waves.

King's Lynn began as a small trading settlement in the corner of The Wash which the Romans found a useful landing despite the shifting sandbars. The small rivers Nar and Wissey vented there, and not far north was the little river Babingley which came down from another tiny Saxon port at Castle Rising. To the south of what was then a wide estuary was a large area of salt lakes and marshes, and salt in mediaeval times was a very valuable resource. It was essential for the preservation of meat and fish, and salt production undoubtedly helped the fledgling settlement to thrive.

However, it was not until the Babingley dried up, and the great River Ouse shifted its course to flow through Lynn that the struggling settlement really began to flourish and developed into the fourth largest port in England. The Wash ports of Boston and

Lynn were ideally placed to trade with Northern Europe, and were only below London and Southampton among the great ports of England.

THE KING'S LYNN WATERFRONT AT PURFLEET QUAY

Medieval Lynn grew rich on the wool trade and from corn, and incoming timber and furs. Later the town benefited from the Icelandic fisheries, and to a lesser degree from the Greenland whale fishing. King John united the settlements on both sides of the river with a charter in 1204 and later, in the 14th century, the great North German Hanseatic League of Merchants had a trading centre and warehouses here. The quaysides at Lynn were jam-packed with ships, and the skyline became a swaying forest of tall masts and rigging. Originally it was called Bishop's Lynn, but Henry VIII changed its name to King's Lynn after the Dissolution.

Today's King's Lynn is still a busy port, and due to its long maritime heritage is still a fascinating town to visit and explore. Most of the cod and herring fishing has now disappeared, but there are still a few net-draped boats, and cockles, mussels and shrimps are still harvested in The Wash. The town still has cobbled yards, old merchants houses and warehouses, two ancient guildhalls, a three hundred year-old custom house, the ruined tower of the old Greyfriars Church, and the magnificent twin west towers of 12th century St. Margaret's.

BURNHAM OVERY
WINDMILL
DOMINATES THE
SKYLINE OVER THE
SURROUNDING
MARSHES

To the north, along The Wash shore is Hunstanton, unique in East Anglia in that it faces west, and is the only place where you can sit on the greensward above vivid red and brown striped cliffs and watch the seagulls fly against the sun sinking slowly into the sea. New Hunstanton was developed in Victorian and Edwardian times as one of the newly popular seaside resorts, thanks to its safe bathing beaches and the advent of the railways. Old Hunstanton was once a fishing village where the boats were beached, but never a port. But swing east, around the north coast, and there are a string of places which once had small quays and saw their fair share of trade in the Middle Ages.

Burnham Overy Staithe still has a crumbling brick and concrete loading wharf, although the last regular sea trade died out when the railway came to Wells in 1857. The original wooden quays were probably established around 1400 when the little river Burn silted up and was no longer navigable up to the old port at Burnham Overy. Now the tidal creek that winds out through mud banks and salt marsh to the sea, is visited mostly by small yachts and pleasure boats.

WELLS HARBOUR IS STILL BUSY WITH SMALL SHIPS

The whole area is now part of the Holkham National Nature Reserve, a wildlife habitat of marshland, reed beds and narrow waterways, the banks filled with oyster catchers, avocets and shellduck digging their beaks into the soft, silvery mud. The white-sailed windmill on the skyline is a backdrop for flights of geese, lapwings and swans.

Moving east, past a magnificent four-mile beach and a coast-line backed with pine woods and sand dunes, is the thriving little seaside resort and port of Wells. It began as a small Danish settle-ment in a sheltered bay at the mouth of little river Stiffkey around 900 AD. In those days small ships could get inland as far south as Walsingham, and would have carried goods and pilgrims down to the great Abbey Shrine.

BLAKENEY, A POPULAR PORT OF CALL FOR YACHTSMAN AND PLEASURE CRAFT

The town and harbour is about a mile back from the deep tidal channel which connects it to the sea. Small coasters still tie up below the grain silo and fishing boats line the quay. Yachts and sailing dinghies are plentiful, afloat or drawn up on the mudflats. With the white wings of gulls and terns wheeling and gleaming in a gold-bronze sunset, and red and silver spangles glittering on the waters, this is as charming a place as anywhere on a high summer evening.

SMALL CRAFT
LINE THE INNER
REACHES OF THE
CREEK AT
BLAKENEY

Blakeney, tucked behind the long curving shingle spit of Blakeney Point, runs it a close second. A rival harbour and one of the small group of thriving wool ports around the original Glaven estuary in the Middle Ages, Blakeney is the most picturesque coastal village of them all. Now a popular sailing centre, the harbour and the main channel to the sea will be filled with masts and sails when there is any sort of breeze short of a full gale.

From here you can take a walk around the salt marshes and the sea wall to the handsome landmark of Cley Windmill. Cley was also a busy mediaeval port, but declined with the arrival of the railways in the middle of the 19th century. Where once the estuary was busy with trade and shipping, there are now more water meadows, reed beds and marshland. Cley has not seen the sea since the disastrous flood tides of 1953 brought the waves briefly crashing back to the base of the windmill.

Sherringham and Cromer, the two major holiday resorts on the north Norfolk coast, are both built high on crumbling cliffs. Small fishing villages first appeared here, clusters of cottages above the cliffs, with the boats drawn up on the beaches below. There are still boats on the shingle and sand, and both resorts are famous for their crabs and lobsters.

From the sea, Sheringham presents an almost castle-like defensive ziggurat of stone breakwaters and concreted cliff faces holding up the esplanades and the attractive red-roofed town. In the centre of the town there is a convenient natural gap in the cliffs, which was once the main access to the mostly shingle beach. Here the original fishing settlement first evolved from the first crude huts where the fishermen stored their gear. Longshore fishing for cod and mackerel, skate and whiting kept almost 150 boats employed by the middle of the 19th century.

With the arrival of the railways and the new fashion for sea bathing and a day at the seaside, Sherringham blossomed with the new town above the cliffs. The charming little Poppy Line is still preserved, with old-fashioned steam engines still pulling trains between Sherringham, Weybourne and Holt. The timetable is delightfully colour coded, to show regular services during the summer months of July and August, but reduced services in spring and autumn.

Cromer is only a short distance away, a bracing 5 mile walk over the cliff tops and along the beach. As you ascend above Sherringham to Beeston Hill there are fine views along the coast and back over the town. The half-way mark is West Runton, where the Caravan parks spill along the cliff top. On one memorable evening walk I saw a small, almost circular cloud passing above the tower of West Runton church. The last touch of the dying sun turned it into a halo of gold, a fitting and haunting image.

Cromer is in many ways similar to Sherringham, a Victorian town of fine houses and hotels rising above the cliffs and promenades, dominated by the massive church tower of St. Peter and St. Paul. The church tower is the tallest in Norfolk and still a landmark for sailors and fishermen, although the fine modern pier with its amusements and theatre also help to make Cromer unmistakable.

Like Sherringham, Cromer has a natural gap in the cliffs, here known as The Gangway, which became the centre of the town. There was an original town called Shipden, which vanished more than a thousand years ago beneath the sea. The fishing community that became modern Cromer appeared on the beach in mediaeval times, and the town was granted a charter for a Friday market and a yearly fair in 1285. Merchants traded from the beach until the middle of the 19th century, and the rivalry between Cromer and Sherringham fishermen became almost legendary.

Both towns, because of their long association with the sea, have become home to lifeboat stations. The full story of ships and lives saved in storm-lashed seas would fill another book, but it would be unthinkable to leave Cromer without mentioning the name of Henry Blogg, Coxswain of the Cromer Lifeboat, who is credited with helping to save the lives of 873 men and women and children, and one dog. His incredible story is fully told in an exhibition in the old lifeboat house, and he is honoured with a bronze bust in North Lodge Park.

SOUTH QUAY LINED WITH SHIPS FOR THE GREAT YARMOUTH MARITIME FESTIVAL

Now we have left behind the sand dunes, marshy creeks and disappearing estuaries, and the shoreline has changed to a continuing succession of long narrow beaches below sea-battered cliffs. There are virtually no more river mouths between here and Great Yarmouth, and the tiny sea-facing villages were generally only beach landings for inshore fishermen. Much of this coastline is still disappearing, with cliff-faces sliding beneath the waves as the storms and gales still pound in from the wild North Sea. Millions of pounds have been spent on sea defences such as the concrete reefs at Sea Palling, but for many it is still a story of too little, too late.

Caister once had a Roman township and harbour on the six-mile wide estuary of the combined rivers Bure, Yare and Waveny, but now nothing remains. Modern Caister on Sea with its wide sandy beaches is mainly a holiday resort extension of Great Yarmouth. Over two millennium the once great estuary has dwindled to the relatively narrow mouth of the Yare on the far side of its sand-and-fun-city neighbour.

Yarmouth grew on a sandbank that first divided the estuary in two. As the sandbank became an island and then part of the mainland, Yarmouth developed also in size and importance. At first it was a Saxon settlement taking advantage of the vast shoals of herring that appeared in the North Sea every autumn. This annual silver harvest fuelled the town's growth until it also became a port and ship-building centre to rival Lynn. The shrinking of the inland rivers which curtailed the sea-going traffic into Norwich also diverted ships and trade to Yarmouth.

In the 12th century vast amounts of wool were being shipped out of Yarmouth, and by the 15th century the merchants of the Hanseatic League had also moved in to set up their own warehouse. Like Lynn the stone quays of Yarmouth were bustling with commerce and lined with high-mast sailing ships. Yarmouth was closer than London to Rotterdam and the town grew wealthy on its trading links with the continent. Later, in the 18th century, came the second great peak in the herring fishery.

Today Great Yarmouth is the pleasure capital of Norfolk, catering mainly to holiday-makers with five miles of promenade entertainments and golden beaches. However, its heritage is still preserved around the old north and south quays, still half circled by its medieval town walls and towers.

Remember that all this did not exist two thousand years ago. The Norfolk shore continues to be at the mercy of the elements of the great North Sea, and with the advent of global warming some forecasts predict that there will be even greater changes to the shape of our coastline in the future. It is a sobering thought but one thing is certain, that this glorious Norfolk shore will always be home to sailors, fishermen, seagulls and wildfowl, and to its own fascinating maritime heritage. Perhaps the only lesson is to enjoy the stunning beauty of the red sand cliffs, the yellow sand beaches and the wild, wet marshes, as they are today.

AT KING'S LYNN THERE ARE STILL A FEW FISHING BOATS AT BOAL QUAY

AT LOWESTOFT FISH FAYRE, FRAMED IN FLAGS, ROPES, AND CABLES,
THE SMALL CRAFT WERE CONSTANTLY CIRCLING THE HARBOUR

SAVING SOULS

5

5   SAVING SOULS

In the glorious heyday of the Norfolk herring fishing in the latter part of the 19th century there were around 12,000 fishermen and boys working in the gale-lashed waters of the harsh North Sea. The boats sailed and fished in fleets of fifty or more smacks and trawlers, and could be away for two months at a time. They trawled at night, hauled up the catch around dawn, and then transferred it to faster carrier boats which then raced the ice-packed silver harvest to port where it could be sold as quickly and as fresh as possible. The fishing fleet stayed out in the cold, grey wastes of water to carry on their hard and freezing tasks of trawling and hauling.

It was a cruel, harsh life, with men frequently washed overboard and lost in the vicious gales, or during the dangerous task of transferring the laden fish boxes from one boat to another. On average a fisherman was lost at the rate of one a day during the decade from 1880 to 1890. Accidents, sickness and injuries were common, and in the early days there was little or no medical help or relief.

Then in 1881 Ebenezer Mather, the secretary of a church mission on the Thames was asked if anything could be done to help the fishermen on the North Sea. Mather responded by personally visiting the fishing grounds, and was appalled by what he saw. The fleet he first encountered consisted of almost two hundred fishing smacks, containing up to a thousand men and boys. He likened it to a floating village, but without the benefits of a school or a hospital, not even a dispensary, or even a church.

And so began the story of what was to become the Royal National Mission to Deep Sea Fishermen, and the long and gallant line of the mission ships, or the bethel ships, as they were also known. There were twenty of them sailing over a period of almost seventy years between 1882 and 1950. They sailed under their own proud blue flag, with their principles scrolled across their bows in the simple promise to PREACH THE WORD and HEAL THE SICK, and they were literally a Godsend to the forgotten fishermen of the North Sea.

The first mission smack was the 56-ton yawl-rigged smack *Ensign*, later re-named the *Thomas Grey*, which was built by Fellows at Southtown, Great Yarmouth, and sailed on her first mission voyage from Gorlestone in 1882. She carried bibles and warm woollen clothing to give away, plus a well stocked medicine chest. Also on board were Ebenezer Mather, to preach the word, and a doctor to heal the sick and injured.

One boat owner was recorded as saying that his men were, "Out there to catch fish, and not sing Hallelujahs!" But most fishermen were devout believers, and the sailing and arrival of the *Ensign* was greeted with more cheers than jeers. Many skippers would not sail on a Sunday, and if they were at sea they would not fish on the Lord's day. Now they had a definite focus and source of encouragement, and if the Sunday weather permitted the whole fleet would gather as close as possible around the mission ship to sing hymns and listen to Mather's preaching.

On a calm day with a soft breeze, with a host of fishing smacks flocked and circled around the *Ensign*, and hundreds of voices raised in heartfelt prayer and praise, the experience must have been inspirational indeed. Many a man was moved to stand up and declare himself for Jesus, and generally his shipmates respected him for it.

The first mission boat had been purchased with a generous donation from a gentleman benefactor, but although the mission continued to receive voluntary help from a great many private sources, there was still not enough to fund all its work.

The only way to continue was to fit the continuing line of mission vessels for trawling, so that in addition to their mission and medical work they could also help to pay their way by actually fishing alongside the boats they had come to serve. It was a move that even further endeared them to the fishermen of the North Sea. The mission ships and their crews not only preached to them and prayed with them, they actually shared in the back-breaking day to day toil of casting and hauling the nets.

In addition to his missionary and medical work, Mather was able to perform one more huge service to the fishermen, and that was to get them out of the clutches of the unscrupulous copers. The name coper came from the Dutch word 'Kooper', meaning to barter, and was bestowed upon the Dutch traders who preyed upon the fishing fleets selling poisonous liquor and foul tobacco. As the fishermen spent some 300 days per year at sea they had no choice but to pay the extortionate prices demanded by the copers, often selling all but their souls for the small comforts that were all but killing them.

Mather persuaded the British Government to sell him tobacco and then allow him to sell it on duty-free to the fishermen at sea. The move caused outrage among some of the more rigid prohibitionists on shore, but it undercut the copers and drove them out of business.

The mission ships too were prey to the toll of the sea, and in all seventeen men were lost at sea. One later vessel, the hospital steamer *Strathcona* lost power and sank off Newfoundland in 1922, although in this instance there was a passing schooner near enough to answer her distress call and save her crew.

Initially all the work of the mission to deep sea fishermen was based at Gorleston, on the south side of the Yare river mouth opposite Great Yarmouth. Six of the early mission vessels were built and launched at Great Yarmouth between 1882 and 1891.

The first mission shoreworker was appointed in Gorleston in 1890. A mariner's refuge was opened in Gorleston in 1896, in the same year a fisherman's bethel opened in Pier Walk. Finally in 1898 the Jubilee Institute in Gorleston High Street opened as the Mission HQ as the on-going work expanded. By then Her Majesty Queen Victoria was a patron of the mission.

THE QUEEN'S MEMORIAL BUILDING, THE JUBILEE INSTITUTE, THE MISSION HQ FROM 1898 TO 1949 AT THE TOP OF GORLESTON HIGH STREET

There were eight mission smacks, one after another, working alongside the fleets, and then in 1888 the 9th mission vessel was the *Queen Victoria,* the first purpose built hospital ship on the North Sea. At 152 tons she was almost 100 foot in length, and carried a ward with eight beds and two swing cots. She was followed over the years by two more hospital smacks and four hospital steamers.

The twentieth and last mission vessel finally exited the service in 1950. Times were changing, the herring and the great fishing fleets that sailed to catch them were disappearing, and the mission ships themselves were no longer needed. However, by this time the mission was firmly shore-based with institutes, homes and centres in every major fishing port around the British Isles. The magnificent work had also been extended to Ireland and to Greenland, Labrador and Newfoundland.

The continuing work of the mission is all shore-based now. The original Gorelston buildings are all closed or gone, but the spiritual and human welfare care of all fishermen still working along the East Anglian coast, from Aldeborough to The Wash, is maintained from the Mission Centre at Lowestoft, just over the county border in Suffolk, where I spoke to Mission Superintendent Keith Rains.

"As the years have gone on we have moved further away from God," he said sadly. "It's as simple as that. But the mission has now adapted to the changing needs. There's no longer a need to provide the mission ships, or even bed and breakfast for crews on shore, but now we do much more welfare work. It is part of a fisherman's basic character that they and their families are very self-sufficient and independent, and when it comes to hardship they still tend to look after themselves and each other, and not realize what other help is available.

"So we are still here to help out in times of trouble. We have people all around the coast who will ring me whenever they hear of a problem, or there is a death or some other tragedy. We help in different ways, but the concept and the principles on which the mission was founded are still unchanged. We still hold services across all Christian denominations.

"We've seen big changes in the fishing industry around our coast-line, but whether there is a big industry or not there will always be some level of fishing. There are now only about seven beam trawlers fishing out of Lowestoft, and only a few boats fishing out of Gorleston and Yarmouth. Further up there are the crab fishermen at Cromer and Sherringham, and then the shell fishermen around The Wash. The fishing industry has always been up and down. Even in 1881 when Ebenezer Mather was looking for funds to buy the second mission ship, he thought that fishing was in decline, and he was not sure how long the industry would survive. So nothing changes. However many fishermen there are, we will always be here for them."

AT LOWESTOFT FISH
FAYRE *THE DEFENDER*
WAS OPEN TO THE
PUBLIC

The Royal National Mission to Deep Sea Fishermen is a registered charity and receives no help from the government. It is totally funded by private donations and, although the great age of the mission ships has gone, the mission work continues. The North Sea is a horrendous place to work in some of the hardest waters in the world, and most of us still like to see fish on our plates.

AT LOWESTOFT FISH FAYRE, A LINE OF FISHING CRAFT ALONGSIDE CORYESTES

One way in which money is raised, and which also provides a unique opportunity to appreciate the fishing heritage of the Norfolk and Suffolk coastline is the annual Lowestoft Fish Fayre. For one day of the year, usually in mid-summer, the quaysides of the Waveny Road wet dock will be lined with all kinds of vessels associated with the fishing industry, while small smacks and fishing boats will be proudly circling the harbour. There will be shanty men singing their lusty mix of sail-raising and capstan-hauling traditional work songs, as well as a whole host of port-side trade and demonstration stalls, craft stalls, and all the usual entertainment associated with any festival fun day.

THE NEW CEFAS ENDEAVOUR, A STATE OF THE ART RESEARCH SHIP

The Fish Fayre is firmly focussed on the glorious heritage of fishing but does not ignore the continuing work of the fishing community, or related areas of ongoing ocean work. One of the regular attendances is by CEFAS, the Centre for Environment, Fisheries and Aquaculture Science, which has one of its three coastal laboratories based in Lowestoft. When possible one of its research vessels will be one of the major attractions of the day, perhaps *Coryestes*, with more than 35 years of scientific research work behind her, or state of the art *Endeavour*, launched in 2003. Both ships concentrate their work on fisheries science advice on the state of fish stocks, ecosystem science and environmental pollution.

The Lowestoft Fish Fayre is just outside of Norfolk, but the fishing fleets knew no county boundary and the Fayre highlights the history and heritage of the Norfolk coast as much as that of Suffolk, and is well worth a visit.

WHERE TWO RIVERS MEET

6

6   WHERE TWO RIVERS MEET

The two rivers are the charming little River Thet and the Little
Ouse. They meet at Thetford to form the south-east border
between Norfolk and Suffolk before joining the Great Ouse at
Brandon Creek, on its northward journey to the sea. The Little
Ouse passes through the dark, deer-haunted forests and the wild
sandy heaths of Breckland, and then into the even more lonely
world of the watery fens, linking two of Norfolk's most exciting
and variable landscapes.

AS THE LIGHT
STARTS TO FADE
OVER THE FENS,
THE LITTLE OUSE
REACHES
BRANDON CREEK

A glance at the map shows a crazy paving pattern of small streams that finally make up the Thet as it flows sedately past the northern outskirts of East Harling, overlooked by the splendid flint tower and lead-covered oak spire of the parish church of St. Peter and St. Paul. A church has stood here since the time of the Conqueror, and the village was famous during the middle ages for its twice yearly, three-day fairs and regular markets. Those are now past, but the village sign today is still a carved wooden lamb, a reminder of the annual sheep fairs that were still being held into the early years of the 20th century.

The Thet has another ten miles to flow, south-east through mainly gentle farmlands, before reaching its historic rendezvous with the Little Ouse. The Ouse has its source in the marshy nature reserve of Lopham Fens and has already served part of its duty as Norfolk's southern border before the two rivers meet in the ancient heart of Thetford. As they come together they pass through the Nunnery Lakes Nature Reserve, where the British Trust for Ornithology has created a network of tiny lakes and islands in an area of sheep-grazed heathland. Here oystercatchers and little ringed plovers can find safe nesting sites. Bird and butterfly life proliferates, and on this stretch of the Thet the patient visitor who can wait for dusk can sometimes catch a glimpse of the nocturnal and reclusive otter.

The town of Thetford owes its history and its origin to its location on this prehistoric crossing point, a ford on the Icknield Way. Like any major line of trade and communication this was also a strategic military point, and was first defended by the construction of an overlooking Iron Age hill fort some 500 years BC. By the time the Romans came the Iceni were the dominant people here, and probably had their tribal centre within the rectangular ditched enclosure of round houses that has been excavated at Gallows Hill.

From here, in 61 AD, Boudicca, the Warrior Queen of the Iceni, launched her initially successful revolt against the Romans. Her husband, Prasutagus, had died the year before, leaving her with two daughters but no male heir. Prasutagus had tried to divide his wealth and his kingdom evenly between his daughters and their Roman masters, but the Roman Governor Paulinus wanted it all. Boudicca was whipped and her two daughters raped for their temerity in trying to hold on to even half of what was rightfully theirs.

The furious Boudicca headed a rebellion at the first opportunity and the twin rivers were slashed with sheeting spray as her army thundered southward, the hooves of their horses and the iron-wheeled, iron-bladed chariots whirling up a maelstrom of froth and foam. Gathering allies on the way the insurgents stormed through Suffolk and Essex and burned Camulodunum, as Colchester was then known. They attacked London, massacred Roman military outposts and cut to pieces the mighty 9th Legion. Hell truly had no fury like this woman scorned. Boudicca seemed unstoppable. Her forces are said to have slaughtered over 70,000 Romans and pro-roman Britons before Paulinus finally raised an army to defeat her in one last desperate battle. Boudicca then took poison and died.

Later, after her eventual defeat and death, the Romans in their turn marched their grim legions north across the twin fords to take their brutal and bloody revenge.

When the initial blood lust was satisfied the Romans ruled more or less peacefully for the next 350 years, then they were recalled to more serious business at home. Angles and Saxon settlers found their way along the rivers, and they and raiding Viking armies filled the gap. Thetford became popular as winter quarters for the Danes, and for fifty years in the late 9th century most of East Anglia was under Viking control.

Finally, the Normans arrived in 1066, and the old hill-top fort and its earthworks and ditches were massively expanded to make the huge, eighty-foot high castle mound into the tallest mediaeval earthwork in Britain. It still survives, as Castle Hill, a much-loved natural adventure playground for children and a scenic viewpoint which still dominates the modern town, but the proud timber castle built on top has long since gone.

William named one of his knights, Ralph Guader, as the new Earl of East Anglia, but Ralph was foolish enough to lead a Barons Revolt against the crown and was soon replaced by the infamous Roger Bigod. The latter was not all-bad, as he did found the magnificent Cluniac Priory which was soon to spread along the riverbank beside the town and become one of Norfolk's premier centres of mediaeval pilgrimage. The ruins today are haunting towers and arches of broken flint which testify a glorious past.

THE OLD COFFEE MILL ON THE THET IN THE HEART OF THETFORD

The twin rivers enter Thetford by passing under the humped stone arches of the Nuns Bridges, so named because nearby there once stood the mediaeval nunnery of St. George. There is a long record of water mills along this stretch of the river, and an old flour mill still stands where the rivers converge just before Button Island. On this shaded little haven you can also find the mounted statue of Duleep Singh, the last Sikh Maharajah of the Punjab, who spent the last years of his life in exile at nearby Elveden.

Not too far away you can find the bronze-gilded statue of Thetford's most famous son, in King Street in front of the 14th century Church of St. Peter.

Thomas Paine was the author of *The Rights of Man*, a defence of the French revolution and republican principles, and *The Age Of Reason*, an exposition of the place of religion in society. He was one of the great political philosophers and thinkers behind the American Revolution.

Paine was born in Thetford in 1737, but his early life in England was not particularly successful. He finally sailed to seek his fortune in the new land of America on the advice of Benjamin Franklin, who gave him letters of introduction. Paine arrived in Philadelphia in 1774. War was in the air with the new American colonists in conflict with England and Paine was soon writing pamphlets arguing for full independence from the parent country. When the war broke out Paine was a volunteer aide-de-camp to General Nathanael Green. He continued to write his soul stirring pamphlets, and George Washington ordered one of them to be read aloud to his troops at their encampment in Valley Forge. It had been a hard winter with the colonist army on the point of disintegration but Paine's words pulled them together. They went on to win the war and the Independence of the United States of America.

Paine returned to England and went on to write his two great books. They brought him both fame and persecution. In England he was found guilty of seditious libel and declared an outlaw. He escaped to France only to be imprisoned there. Finally he was allowed to return to the United States where he died in New York City in 1809. His writings lived on, and the handsome statue that now honours him in Thetford was a gift to the town from the Thomas Paine Foundation of America.

ONE RIVER
NOW, THE
LITTLE OUSE
FLOWS UNDER
THE TOWN
BRIDGE

One river now, the Little Ouse, flows out of Thetford under the Town Bridge, all smartly painted in a livery of red, green and gold. Once a heavily used iron toll bridge it now carries relatively little traffic; the modern bypass that is the A11 sweeps it all away to the north.

We are now moving into the heart of Breckland, 370 square miles of forest, heath and farmland which form a unique natural landscape. This was close to my home territory, where as a boy I have feasted on ripe blackberries and sweet chestnuts and hazel nuts, and plundered the horse chestnut trees for conkers. I have hunted rabbits with a catapult in the heather, beaten the bracken to flush out the game birds for the guns on a pheasant shoot, and stood breathless to watch wild deer grazing at dawn or sunset on the edge of a forest ride. Now there are usually too many people about, walking or riding the forest paths that cut through the long ranks of tall pines, or the smaller glades and pockets of deciduous woods, but much of the old woodland magic is still there.

There is a riverside path all the way down to Brandon. It passes the modern village of Santon Downham, where you can find the District Office of the Forestry Commission which planted all those dominant fir plantations, but on the Norfolk bank you can also find the site of the old village of Santon. It was probably settled on by Vikings in the late 9th century, a small group who either did not quite reach Thetford or else decided that they did not want to be part of that much larger community.

All that remains of the village now are a few grassy humps and hollows to show where a flint hunting lodge once existed within a square moat. It was never more than a tiny hamlet and there would only have been a few small cottages surrounded by a vast, sandy heath, suitable only for grazing sheep and catching rabbits. However, once a year, on the eve of the Nativity of St. John The

Baptist, they did have an annual fair, and they had a church which was one of the smallest in England. The little church was rebuilt in 1628 and is still there, a tiny flint tower of faith, unused now but remaining when all else has vanished into the mists of time.

POSSIBLY THE OLDEST CHURCH IN ENGLAND, THIS TINY, DISUSED CHURCH STANDS BY THE RIVER BANK, WHERE THERE WAS ONCE THE TINY SAXON HAMLET OF SANTON

The source of all those flints is not far from here, at Grimes Graves where over 300 pits were dug in Neolithic times to excavate the axe, spear and arrow heads that stone-age man needed for his tools and weapons. Later flints were mined for building material and Norfolk is full of flint-faced buildings, from small country cottages and barns to great, towering churches. The flints were knapped, that is broken open to give them a flat polished face.

Then there was a thriving industry for the manufacture of gun flints for the first muskets, especially during the Napoleonic wars.

Of more than a hundred collapsed pit hollows in the area, only one 30-foot deep pit is now open to the public. It is now an English Heritage site with a Visitor Centre and admission charges. Much more informative I am sure, but when I was boy we could sneak down and crawl up some of the galleries where generations before us had burned their names and initials on to the white chalk walls with candle flames. Now all the galleries have iron grille gates to keep small boys and casual explorers out.

WEETING, AND THE LONGEST SINGLE ROW OF THATCHED COTTAGES IN ENGLAND

The nearest village is Weeting, another tiny Saxon settlement where the small, 11th century church can be seen framed between the crumbled flint walls which are all that remain of moated Weeting castle. The row of eight, white-painted, thatched cottages beside the village green is said to be the longest single thatch cottage row in England.

Weeting is still on the doorstep of the Breckland forests, but move along the Ouse valley to Hockwold and we are entering the world of the fens. There are many more flint-walled cottages here, especially around the green, where a large and lovely red-flowering chestnut tree is planted in commemoration of the Jubilee of King George V. Hockwold is a name derived from a word meaning a religious meeting place in a wood, and beside the tree a symbolic stone cross is believed to mark the ancient spot.

HOCKWOLD, A CHARMING VILLAGE GREEN, WITH THE
JUBILEE CHESTNUT AND THE HOCKWOLD CROSS FLANKED BY
TRADITIONAL FLINT COTTAGES AND A FLINT PUB

The rest of the river's journey is through Fenland, under open skies where kestrels hunt and skylarks soar. Once fishing and wildfowling were the only ways of life in this watery world, but now the river is almost entirely the haunt of weekend fishermen, match-fishing for pike, roach and bream. Finally the Little Ouse flows into the Great Ouse, and like the Thet gives up its own identity.

THE GREAT OUSE – A
FENLAND RIVER

7

7 THE GREAT OUSE – A FENLAND RIVER

The Great Ouse is a majestic river, it flows out of Cambridgeshire and enters Norfolk in the south-west corner of the county, there to flow deep and wide through the Norfolk Fenlands, under vast flatland skyscapes, where on a fine day the clouds can pile up in fantastic white-froth swirls of baroque cumulus. It exits through salt marsh and glistening tidal mud flats into the great square sea-bite of The Wash, where the hungry North Sea heaves and waits.

GREYLAG GEESE PARADE ALONG THE GRASSY RIVER BANK

The river begins the Norfolk leg of its journey at Brandon Creek, a waterway junction where it is joined by the Little Ouse, which forms part of Norfolk's border with Suffolk. In mediaeval times the rivers were always the main avenues of movement and transport through the wet marshlands, and every junction was a meeting place and a port of call. Today's river travellers are mostly pleasureboat owners, with a leavening of fishermen dreaming of fat bream, giant pike and sporting zander, and they are still served their ale in the historic Ship Inn, which has stood here since the middle of the 17th century.

The Ship was originally built to house some of the great workforce of labourers brought in by the group of investors headed by the Fourth Duke of Bedford to dig out the Old Bedford River. They put into action the heroic scheme designed by the Dutch engineer Cornelius Vermuyden to drain 190,000 acres of the fens. The Old Bedford River was 70 feet wide and 21 miles long, slashing a perfectly straight diagonal line across the fens from Cambridgeshire into Norfolk. The fen floods were hard to beat and twenty years later a second man-made river, the New Bedford River, was dug parallel to the first.

The land in-between the two rivers, known as the Hundred Foot Washes, was allowed to flood in winter and then drained in summer to provide first class grazing pasture. It was the most ambitious project yet conceived in the long history of man's efforts to tame the vast expanse of bleak and waterlogged marshes that were best suited to wildfowl, eels and fish.

The Ship Inn has another ghoulish claim to fame in its own ghost story. A group of soldiers caught up in lust and drink had violated the wife and daughter of a former landlord. They were pursued and apprehended, and paid a dreadful punishment. They were buried up to their necks in the mud of the riverbank, and left to drown slowly as the tide rose and the river claimed them.

After the event the landlord was seized by remorse and it is his guilt-ridden ghost that on a misty, moonless night, is said to still haunt the riverbank.

Further down the river are the great iron and concrete sluices at Denver, where the Old and the New Bedford Rivers drain into the Great Ouse, and a new relief channel begins that was cut to parallel the remaining course of the main river to The Wash and the sea. In addition to these four main waterways there are three more rivers that meet at or near this Fenland version of a wet Spaghetti Junction. The 18th and 19th centuries saw more gigantic projects to fight the Fenland floods, and now there are five great sets of sluice gates here to control the combination of drainage waters and riverflow.

In all it took some three hundred years to create a system which could drain the fens effectively. Initially the surplus drainage water was simply vented into the sea. Then in the 1960s it was realized that the excess water could be used in Essex where there was a shortage and the county reservoirs were half empty. A cut off channel had already been created to drain the excess waters of the Little Ouse, the Lark and the Wissey, and by reversing the flow here the water could be redirected back to the south.

The diversion sluice that now stands astride the cut-off channel does exactly that, and beyond the cut-off channel a twenty mile tunnel and then a pipeline now takes Norfolk's excess water on a 140 kilometer journey to where it is needed.

Denver sluice is the ideal point to start a walk along the riverbank and absorb some of that magnificent panorama of river and sky. Upstream of the sluices there are sheltered moorings for pleasure boats along the bank, and small yachts and white-sailed dinghies skittering about on the water. There is a sailing club here and the popular Jenyns Arms pub. A couple of miles upriver along the riverbank will take you to the junction of the incoming River Wissey, or your can walk downriver to Downham Market.

THE PEACEFUL RIVER OUSE BY DENVER SLUICE

I chose the latter route on a spring morning with snow-clean clouds piled high in the blue sky, and a fresh breeze playing along the top of the high bank where the path followed the course of the river. The Great Ouse flowed on my left and on my right, beyond low flat water meadows, the relief channel. The brown tower and white sails of Denver Mill, still a working windmill, stood small but dominant upon the horizon. Downham Market lay ahead, a smudge of houses behind a vista of meadows and hedgerows.

On a bleak day it might have been a desolate walk, but with the sun shining there were endless points of interest. The mud banks steamed like molten silver and along the top of the far bank there were flashes of white May blossom and bleating sheep with new born lambs. One tiny black lamb, perhaps delighting in being different, seemed to be leaping higher than all the others. A sparrowhawk wheeled high in the sky. Where there were low trees there were rooks and magpies. Wild geese were streamlining down into the water. The Fen Rivers Way, marked for walkers, runs all the way from Brandon Creek to Downham Market and this was a breath-taking sample.

Downham Market is one of Norfolk's oldest market towns and dates back to Saxon times. Slightly raised it was once an island only just clear of the flood levels of the Great Ouse, which runs side by side with the new relief channel along its western edge. Now that the floods are tamed this is a busy little town serving the small villages to the east and the fertile farmlands to the west. In the 19th century it was a centre for Saint Winnold's Horse Fairs, which attracted buyers from as far away as Europe.

ST. MARY MAGDALENE, THE 15TH CENTURY CHURCH AT WIGGENHALL

Its most famous landmark is the Jubilee Clock, a gothic tower smartly painted in black and white which stands in the bustling Market Square. Behind it stands the Town Hall, built in 1887 of yellow brick and brown carstone. The softly mellowed carstone was used in many of the town's fine old buildings, and earned Downham Market its nickname of 'The Gingerbread Town'.

AT WIGGENHALL ST. GERMAN THE CHURCH STANDS CLOSE BY THE RIVER, WITH THE DERELICT TOWER OF ST. PETER JUST VISIBLE ON THE HORIZON

Moving on toward the sea the river flows past the pretty little village of Wiggenhall St. Mary, named after the splendid church dedicated to St. Mary Magdalene. There are actually four Wiggenhalls, a cluster of tiny Fenland villages with each one named after its church. Wiggenhall St. German straddles the river where the church tower snuggles up to the high east bank just below the bridge. Looking upstream from the bridge the church tower of derelict St. Peter is just visible in its lonely isolation, a short walk of a mile or two along the bank. There are many church and mill towers that prick the vast Fenland skies, as though pointing up to the huge blue emptiness, and the ruined tower of St. Peter's is more poignant than most.

Finally the Great Ouse flows into King's Lynn, still a vital port and a vibrant town, although its great days of mediaeval supremacy are gone. However, fishing boats draped with drying nets still tie up at Boal Quay and small snapshots remain of past glories. Here you can still find time-weathered old merchants houses, a 15th century Hanseatic warehouse and cobbled streets. The splendid high-standing ruin of Greyfriars tower is all that remains of the ancient Greyfriars church.

THE WATERFRONT AT KING'S LYNN

The best views of the Kings Lynn waterfront are those from across the river. The ferry will still take you across from Ferry Lane, and a walkway along the west bank takes you to a viewpoint opposite Purfleet Quay and the Old Custom House. This was once the busiest quayside in Lynn, and for three hundred years the prominent landmark of the white timber lantern tower overlooked the coming and going of ships and sailors. Now the Custom House is a Tourist Information Centre, and the quay empty except for the solemn statue of Captain George Vancouver, born in Lynn in 1757, who in 1792 began a three year survey of the coastline of British Columbia, and eventually gave his name to Canada's third largest city.

THE OLD CUSTOM
HOUSE AT KING'S
LYNN, WITH THE
STATUE OF
CAPTAIN GEORGE
VANCOUVER

Also dominant on the riverfront skyline are the twin towers of St. Margaret's church which also dates back to the 12th century. Beside the west door between the two towers are some carved horizontal marks that tell more of the story of the Fenland floods. Each one marks a high tide level when the Great Ouse has overflowed its banks and invaded the town. The dates are 1883, the great tidal surge of 1953, and 1978.

A few more miles and the Great Ouse empties into the south-eastern corner of The Wash, although as we have seen, this is a two-way flow. It can be a treacherous place of fast rising tides and quicksands, as King John found to his cost when he tried to make a short cut crossing with his royal baggage train in 1216. This was one of those turbulent times in mediaeval history when England was again in the throes of civil war. The barons had forced John to sign the Magna Carta at Runnymede, but the tricky King regarded this as just a way of buying time and was still trying to scheme a way out of his obligations. Realizing that John meant to break their contract and had no real intention of implementing its reforms, the Barons were again in rebellion. Because he was surrounded by enemies, John kept his royal treasure with him and when he attempted to cross The Wash he was caught by the incoming tide and lost it all, barely escaping with his own life.

Here today there are shifting sandbanks and a desolate shoreline of mud and salt marsh that is home only to a vast variety of waterfowl. The Wash can be deceptively calm and peaceful, or a fury of wind and waves when the gales are blowing. It can be as changeable as the great Fenland river we have just traversed, as hauntingly beautiful or as wild and lonely, depending on its mood.

WANDERING THE WENSUM

8

8 WANDERING THE WENSUM

The Wensum flows in a shallow, winding valley that rises gently in two streams west and south of Fakenham. The little Tat, which meets the Wensum at Tatterford, is one; the other is the Wensum itself which rises to flow between the two villages of East and West Raynham. After a short northward loop the river flows past Fakenham and then it is a diagonal wriggle, south-east all the way to Norwich.

SMART MODERN HOUSING, WITH NEATLY TRIMMED LAWNS,
SWEEPING DOWN TO THE RIVER AT FAKENHAM

Fakenham, 'The Fair Place On The River', was named by the first Saxons to settle here, probably around the end of the 6th century. By the time the Domesday Book was written it had a recorded population of 150, but later it became a thriving market town, gaining advantage from its choice location between the great country estates of Holkham, Houghton and Raynham. Here the Agricultural Revolution was born, and Fakenham prospered with it.

In the mid 19th century there was a flourishing printing industry here, rivalling the cattle and sheep fairs as a source of income. Today it is all commemorated in a remarkable series of cast iron plaques set into the ancient market square in front of the town's war memorial, overlooked by a set of fine old Georgian buildings and the lofty square flint tower of the parish church of St. Peter and St. Paul.

FAKENHAM
TOWN CENTRE

A walk along Hall Staithe will take you down to the river. A side stream here was once the river access into the town. Graceful old willows line the main riverbank and a few steps upstream is a bridge that will take you to the far bank. Walk downstream again and you will soon find a fine open view of the church and town, nestling under trees across the river valley. Not far beyond there are some attractive modern houses lining the opposite bank, all smart flint and red brick, with flower beds and mani-cured green lawns running right down to the river's edge.

Once there were three mills along the river but now the river walk takes you past only one, a white boarded water mill, still looking the part although it has now been converted into a hotel. The bridge here was built in 1883 after a visit by Queen Victoria left a few red faces when her carriage became stuck in the ford. Never again, the good townsfolk vowed, and so they built the bridge. However, the ruffled monarch still refrained from making a return visit.

THE WENSUM VALLEY, JUST BELOW FAKENHAM

The river swings away from the town, the path crosses the river again and continues to follow its willow-shaded, meandering course. Here was the essence of peaceful tranquility, disappearing through cool tunnels of leaf and water. On my walk I saw no fishermen and not a single boat, the placid surface was the domain of a few mallard and the occasional moorhen. Eventually an out-of-place, three arch Victorian bridge marked the place where the railway line once ran from East Dereham to Wells.

Further down the valley the Wensum passes through Pensthorpe Lakes, now a 500 acre waterfowl and wildlife reserve. Plenty of visitors here, for this is a walker and bird-watcher's paradise, with miles of footpaths wandering around the lakes, through woodlands and wild flower fen meadows. A huge variety of summer breeding birds and winter migrants are drawn to this carefully restored and preserved, natural wetland habitat. Nesting islands have been provided, together with perching points for kingfishers and shallow beaches for waders. In spring and summer dragonflies and butterflies abound.

At North Elmham the emphasis shifts from the glories of nature back into the realms of history, for this is the site of the first Anglo-Saxon cathedral in East Anglia. However, the original cathedral was built of timber, and the broken walls of time-ravaged flint that remain are part of a much later Norman chapel, which then became a fortified manor house. They stand within the remnants of earthworks and ditches that are now grassed over and shaded by trees.

The original timber building served as the first cathedral of East Anglia until 1071. The Diocese headquarters was then transferred to Thetford by Bishop Herfast, who intended the move to be only his first step toward taking over the rich and magnificent monastery at Bury St. Edmunds. He was thwarted by the Abbot at Bury who persuaded the King to grant him independence from the bishops. So the new cathedral remained in Thetford until 1094, when Bishop Herbert de Losinga decided to move his principle seat to Norwich.

However, the Bishops retained a palace and a large estate at Elmham, and on the site of the old wooden cathedral a private stone chapel was eventually built in the 11th century. Then, in the 14th century, the chapel was converted into virtually a castle for Henry le Despencer, who was then Bishop of Norwich.

No doubt the good bishop felt the need for strong defences in face of the general hatred he had earned for leading the merciless suppression of the Peasant's Revolt. The imposition of a poll tax of one shilling a head on every man and woman had enraged the whole country, and led to violent riots in Norwich. The Bishop had restored order and had sentenced the leader of the Norwich rebels to the barbarous punishment of being hung, drawn and quartered. His only concession to the gentilities of his Christian faith was to listen to the man's confession before marching him to the gallows.

His new building at Elmham had towers either side of the entrance and a drawbridge over the encircling dry ditch. The remains of the two towers are still distinguishable, even to the difference in the stonework which indicates that one is a later addition to the other.

Moving downstream the mood changes again to prehistoric fantasy. At Lenwade is Norfolk's answer to Jurassic Park, a Lost World Adventure Zone where dinosaurs rear out from the woodlands and giant predatory birds lurk in the tree branches. Fortunately it only looks real, but take a couple of three to ten year-olds to capture the full spirit and excitement of the place.

The Wensum wanders on and at Ringland we are back to the serenity of nature once more. The village and the river valley are well hidden down leafy lanes, and it is a joy to leave the busy main road. Find the 15th century church of St. Peter and then head up the lane to find Royal Hill. From the summit, reached by a wide farm track, there are splendid views back over the village and down into the Wensum valley.

ON ROYAL HILL, PLOUGH CIRCLES SPIRAL DOWN INTO THE WENSUM VALLEY

I found it when a gusty October wind was blowing and the autumn sunlight gave everything a lovely mellow glow. The fresh ploughed fields made great swirls of brown earth, spiraling down the slopes, west and east into the valley, and on the grassy crest beside the autumn tinted woods yellow cow paisley grew in great clumps. The grey flint tower of the church rose above its green nest of trees, and the air was still and hazy.

The Wensum finishes its course with a lazy loop through the heart of Norwich, before joining with the Yare on its way to the sea. Here we can enter into mediaeval history again and pick up the cathedral story which began in North Elmham. After the See of East Anglia was moved to Norwich in 1096, the building of a magnificent new cathedral was begun, to be finally completed and consecrated in 1278. Again the chosen site was close to the River Wensum, which made for easy transportation of the necessary stone blocks and other materials.

PULL'S FERRY
LEADS YOU
BACK TO THE
WENSUM

At 315 feet the slender stone spire that pierces the skies above Norwich is the second tallest in England. It is actually the fourth of a succession of Norwich cathedral spires. The first was destroyed when part of the cathedral was burned down during an exchange of blazing fire arrows in 1272, the result of riots erupting out of long standing disputes between the townspeople and the monks of the original priory, which still stood in the shadow of the new cathedral. The second spire was blown down by a storm around 1361, and the third was struck by lightning in 1463.

The cathedral's monastic cloisters are the largest in England, the cool tranquility beneath their high arches once felt the soft tread of Benedictine sandals, but are now visited by thousands of tourists. Look up inside the nave and you will see over 250 roof bosses carved with biblical scenes from the creation to the last judgement. There are eleven altars inside this vast edifice to God's glory, and the golden lectern is in the rare form of a pelican feeding her young with the blood from her own breast. Before the High Altar can be found the tomb of Bishop Herbert de Losinga, who began the building work, and behind the High Altar is the Bishop's throne, brought here from the earlier sites and thought to be at least 1,200 years old.

From the cathedral a short walk will take you down to the river, and the low arched brick and flint building that is Pull's Ferry. The archway once spanned the canal that was cut to service the cathedral, but the canal is now filled in. However, once through the archway you are back on the bank of the Wensum. Go upstream to find the lovely old, three-arched Bishop's Bridge, the oldest river bridge in Norwich. Not far beyond the bridge is Cow Tower, a circular red brick tower on a sharp bend of the river that was once part of the city's defences. It was also once a tollhouse for the monks of the old priory who collected revenue from the trade on the river.

THE BISHOP S BRIDGE, THE OLDEST RIVER BRIDGE IN NORWICH

On this stretch of river, between Pull's Ferry and the Bishop's Bridge, there are moored pleasure boats, an indication that our slow and gentle Wensum has at last reached the western edge of busy Broadland. Go on into the Yare and you are into cruising waters.

However, for me the charm of the Wensum lies in its upper reaches, where it wends its way through the green valley without an engine to be heard or a yacht sail to be seen. Where the mallard drift unmolested and the willows weep into the waters. The broads have their place and their attractions but it was nice to find a peaceful contrast.

LULLABY OF BROADLAND

9

9 LULLABY OF BROADLAND

A summer evening on the broads is a magical experience of muted sight and sound. If you are lucky a sunset of flushed pink or rolling gold, but on any calm night a soft lullaby as the day winds down into night. There is an entire orchestra of wind and water, the sighing of the breeze as it rustles through the leaves, and the waving sedges and grasses. There is the creak of sails, the soft chugging of outboard motors as the last boats seek their moorings, the slap of water against hulls and the ripples of the wavelets in the reed beds.

SOMERTON, WHERE STEEL BLADES REPLACE
WOODEN SAILS IN SCYTHING THE SKY

Cows low to their calves on the lonely marshes, disappearing seagulls call goodbye, doves coo, and perhaps the rare boom of the bittern will mingle with the final echoes of birdsong. The last dragonflies and bees will be buzzing home and if you are close to Sommerton the rhythmic *swish, swish* of the great steel sails of the new, modern wind turbines, will add the base drive to the whole dream-like symphony.

Wait for morning and this is as good a place as any to start an exploration of the Northern Broads. As you drive up through Martham to Horsey those magnificent white blades appear repeatedly on the skyline as the road dips up and down, or passes by gaps in the hedgerows, continually circling and slicing the bright blue sky. There are eleven wind turbines in all, two rows of five, and one giant twice as high as all the others standing in a separate field.

HORSEY STAITHE AND WINDPUMP, QUINTESSENTIAL NORFOLK

One of the best places to view them is from the hill-top church-yard by the small round-tower church of St. Mary's at West Sommerton. The round tower has an octagonal upper storey.

From here you can also see the splendid tower of Winterton church, possibly the tallest church tower in Norfolk, and beyond Winterton lie yellow sand dunes and the grey North Sea.

Head north and you will very quickly come to Horsey Mere, the most north-easterly point of that magical network of shallow lakes and linking dykes and rivers that form the Broads. Here stands Horsey Mill, a wind-driven water pump for draining the land, and perhaps the best-known and most photographed survivor of all those hundreds of pumping mills that were once scattered almost as plentifully as oak trees throughout the Norfolk landscape. It stands at the head of Horsey Staithe, a narrow cut leading to the mere, and filled with moored cruisers and sailboats.

Follow the public footpath toward the mere and almost immediately you can see again all those distant white blades scything the skyline, far away behind Horsey Mill. The old and the new standing tall and proud together. More of these majestic new turbines are planned for other parts of Norfolk, and perhaps they will eventually become as commonplace tomorrow as the brick towers and wooden sails of yesterday.

The path from Horsey winds through reed beds, rushes and grasses. Along with farming, reed-cutting for thatch is Horsey's only native industry. The whole area is now a nature reserve, and after crossing fields and marshes the path turns beside a deep dyke of chocolate brown water. When I walked it in midsummer there were tall banks of purple-red foxgloves, alive with drifting bees and butterflies, and creamy-white blackberry blossoms promising an autumn feast for later walkers.

Eventually the single, skeleton sail and the ruined brick tower stump of Boxgrave Mill rose on the opposite bank between the reeds. It is said to be a popular spot for artists, and I could see that its crumbled and haunting beauty would make for some fine atmospheric portraits against a suitable sunset or a stormy-moody sky. For my part I waited in the hope that a trio of swans further downstream would move up into the foreground to make a photograph. They didn't, but then an obliging sail boat came chugging along under motor power with her sail furled. In the Broads, if you have the patience, there will always be a craft of some sort passing eventually to make a picture.

Horsey links to Hickling Broad, the largest but also one of the shallowest of the Broads, where the boat sails were like the heeling white dorsal fins of lazy sharks cutting through the water. Then through Heigham Sound to the little River Thurne. However, the next viewing point for the landlubber is at Potter Heigham with its commercial maze of boatyards and moorings, and boats for hire. Here the river passes under the low single archway of the old, hump-backed stone bridge.

THURNE
DRAINAGE PUMP,
A BROADS
LANDMARK

To find another romantic little staithe, or quayside, go to the tiny riverside village of Thurne. I passed a field of golden sunflowers just before the village and the staithe itself was a delight, the exit to the main river framed between wind pumps. The pristine white Thurne drainage pump on the near bank on the right, and the brown brick tower and full sails of a second pump on the far bank on the left. The path that leads along the river-bank to Potter Heigham is part of the ancient Weaver's Way, which comes up from Yarmouth and the Halvergate marshes, and winds on past Hickling and Stalham to Cromer and the coast.

Just below the village of Thurne the River Thurne flows into the Bure, but follow the Bure upstream for a few twists and turns, and then you can head northward once more along the course of the River Ant. If you are in a car, on a cycle or on foot, your first glimpse of the Ant will probably be from the hump-backed Ludham Bridge, the highpoint of the area, with more boatyards and good views across the windmill sprinkled marshlands beyond.

THE ANT, JUST BELOW LUDHAM BRIDGE

Ludham itself has a splendid Norman church, dedicated to St. Catherine, and there are cream teas available in the thatched row of white cottages opposite the churchyard.

Don't miss How Hill, a few miles up the Ant, with its wildlife trails and nature reserve one of the most beautiful spots in Broadland. The small car park here facing a wide open field, neatly mown like a vast lawn, and on the far side a dip through the trees leads to Toad Hole Cottage, which is now a small museum Immediately beyond is the river bank, with three splendid drainage mills. A hundred yards downstream on the opposite bank is the neat brick tower and white sails of Turf Fen Mill, a lovely sight with moored and passing boats and a trio of swans to decorate the river. While I was there wild flocks of geese took flight overhead from the shallow lagoons behind the reeds.

THE ANT IS NOT
JUST FOR BOATING,
FISHERMEN AND
WALKERS ALSO
ENJOY THE
RIVERBANKS

Just upstream were two skeleton mills, unboarded black timber frames with white caps and sails, and a large pile of cut sedge was drying in the sun beside a small black boathouse. Midsummer is sedge-cutting time, and the sedge is used for roof ridges. The larger reeds used for roof thatch are cut in the winter after the first frosts have killed the reed.

All this I learned in the museum which is set out as it would have appeared as a marshman's cottage in Victorian times, and which tells the story of the marshman's year. In addition to harvesting reed, sedge and marsh hay, the marshmen supplemented their living by catching fish and eels, shooting wildfowl, and caring for cattle and all those drainage mills on the marshes.

Walking back to the car I passed a magnificent Edwardian thatched house which is now a holiday and education centre. I knew Norfolk was rich in thatched cottages and thatch-roofed churches, but this was the size of a small country hall, and a splendid example of the range and diversity of the thatcher's craft.

The Ant flows up through the Reedham Marshes and Barton Broad to Stalham, where another excellent Broads museum is situated on a corner of the old quay. Here you can follow the whole history of the Broads, the hardy people and the shallow boats which worked upon these wild wetlands and mysterious waterways.

While you are this close take a look at the massive, red-brick Sutton Windmill, midway between the Ant and the Thurne, and at nine stories the tallest mill tower in the country. The views from the top are superb. I counted ten church towers through my binoculars, although only three were clearly visible to the naked eye, plus two more old windmill towers. The cap of the windmill behind me was like the up-turned hull of an old clinker-built sailing boat, its faded and peeling blue paint scoured by the weather and wind. The intervening scene beyond the great wooden sails was a green and yellow chequerboard of fields, some with great circular hay bales scattered all around.

TURF FEN MILL AT
HOW HILL

If you have spent a full day exploring along the Ant and the Thurne, then by now the shadows will be lengthening into evening again. We are back to the gentle murmurs of the breeze, and all the soft sighs and tinkles of wind and water. There's a pub at almost every staithe - the Pleasureboat Inn at Hickling, the Lion Inn at Thurne - and as the boats moor up for the night the chink of glasses and the murmurs of conversation and laughter start to replace the last fading chug of engines. It's time to relax, watch the geese fly home against the sunset, and listen to another lullaby of Broadland.

Blue highway

10

10 BLUE HIGHWAY

If Wroxham is the heart of the Broads, then the Bure is its lifeblood, the main artery and living essence of Norfolk's water wonderland. For centuries this sparkling, silver-blue highway has powered mills and carried people and trade through an early wilderness of marshlands that would otherwise have been almost impenetrable. The vast flocks of wildfowl, the abundance of fish and eels, and the easily dug peat fuel to provide household fires for the harsh winters, all helped to make the riverbanks a relatively good place to live in the Middle Ages.

SAILING ON
THE BURE

Square-rigged, single-masted open keel boats plied the river in those early days, slowly to be supplemented and then replaced by the more easily manoeuvrable gaff-rigged wherries. Prior to the First World War there were scores of these lovely old sailing vessels trading along the river, and the upper reaches from Buxton up to Aylsham had been opened up to commercial traffic by the new system of locks and channels around the watermills.

Aylsham takes its name from Aegal's Ham, which in Saxon times meant the homestead of Aegal. It is one of those Norfolk market towns which grew and became prosperous with the wool trade and the manufacture of linens in the Middle Ages. The beautiful flint-faced church of St. Michael still testifies to its wealth and status in its heyday, and its tall tower still dominates the centre of the town. As the wool trade declined corn and timber took its place and Aylsham continued to thrive. It became an important coaching stop between Cromer and Norwich, and throughout those Dickensian days there would be coaches and horses reining up every day outside the Black Boys Inn on the market place.

The 19th century expansion of the roads and railways meant that the rivers were no longer the cheapest and easiest means of transport, and so everything had to change. The commercial river traffic died out, and after suffering severe flood damage in 1912 the Aylsham navigation system beyond Buxton had to be closed.

The northern section of the Bure is now left to walkers along the Bure Valley path, anglers still hauling in the pike, bream and roach along its shaded, overgrown banks, and passengers on the narrow gauge Bure Valley Railway, where steam engines follow the course of the river through some of Norfolk's most beautiful waterway scenery between Aylsham and Hoveton.

THE RISING SUN AT COLTISHALL

Coltishall is now the head of navigation for the bright new world of holiday-makers and pleasure boats that have taken over the Bure and the Broads. There has been a settlement here for a thousand years or more, and the tile evidence suggests that at least one wealthy Roman was enticed into building a lavish villa here. In the 18th century there were eighteen maltings brewing beer and the old boatyards that were once found at Anchor Street were famous for building wherries. The last trading wherry was built here in 1912.

Today there are still some lovely old buildings in the village streets, some with elegant Flemish gables, and on a more modern note the RAF fighter station is only just up the road. However, the heart of Coltishall is still the long stretch of riverside moorings known as the Lower Common. Only the craft have changed, with brightly painted fibreglass hulls and pristine white yacht sails replacing the hard-worked timbers and black-tarred canvas of yesteryear.

Downstream lie Hoveton and Wroxham, twin villages on either side of the Bure. Heart of the Broads, Capital of the Broads, Centre of the Broads, all these titles fit easily on Wroxham, which has been attracting visitors to the Broads for more than sixty years. Once they flooded up from London and Norwich on the railway, or on day-trip coaches from the popular holiday resorts at Yarmouth, Sheringham and Cromer. Now most of them come in their own cars, to spend a day or a week on the water, or simply to watch the regattas on Wroxham Broad.

WROXHAM BRIDGE, WHERE SWANS AND BOATS COMPETE FOR SPACE

Almost all of the constant summertime activity flows over or under the bridge, the boats passing below, and the cars and the pedestrians crossing above.

There are boat hire centres and smart riverfront hotels on either side, and around the bridge itself scores of swans, from pure white adults to fluffy grey cygnets, glide smoothly between the dinghies and cruisers as they flock to be hand-fed at the riverbanks.

THE SWAN HOTEL DOMINATES THE GREEN AT HORNING

The Bure flows on past Salhouse Broad to Horning, a charming riverside village on the north bank with a long waterfront and a wide green where the lovely old black and white timbered Swan Hotel overlooks the river. Here too the old working wherries are long gone, to be replaced by sparkling new motor cruisers and the *Southern Comfort,* a 100 seat, double-deck, Mississippi-style paddle boat that in season cruises up and down the river.

On the opposite side of the river is Woodbastwick, one of the most picturesque little villages in Broadland. It is an estate village almost entirely roofed in reed thatch. The charming little pump house in the centre of the green is thatched and so are all the houses facing the green. The beautiful flint church of St. Fabien and St. Sebastian has a thatched roof. There is even a delightful rambling old thatch roofed pub, the *Fur and Feathers,* which offers a wide range of local Norfolk ales.

THE SOUTHERN COMFORT AT HER MOORINGS IN HORNING

Reed cutting for thatch has long been a traditional Broadland trade, the reed being harder and longer-lasting than straw. The reeds are traditionally cut in February. Once they provided almost the only winter job for the Norfolk fishermen who could not put their boats out into the harsh North Sea during the worst weather of the year. The reeds were sold in fathoms, a six foot measurement round the girth of the bundle that was taken from the more familiar nautical term. It was a hard, wet and cold task but Norfolk reeds were the best and in high demand. Fifty years ago there were extensive reed beds here, regularly harvested from shallow flat-bottomed boats, and today Woodbastwick remains a classic example of a reed-thatched Norfolk village.

ST. BENET'S ABBEY, WHERE AN ABANDONED WINDMILL
WAS BUILT WITHIN THE RUINS OF THE ABBEY GATEWAY

Horning still maintains its long association with what remains of St., Benet's Abbey, only a few twists and turns down the river toward the sea. In the Middle Ages there was a magnificent, two-tower Abbey Church here, founded by Benedictine monks. The Abbey grew rich enough on the lucrative taxes from the extensive peat diggings to attract the attention of the Vikings, who sacked it around 870 AD. King Canute later had it restored and it grew to be one of the largest and most influential monasteries in East Anglia. However, ultimately its huge expenses and spiralling debts caused it to decline. It escaped the Dissolution only because King Henry united the Abbacy with the Bishopric of Norwich, and the Abbey itself was allowed to fall into decay. Eventually it was abandoned and the last monks sadly walked away.

Today all that remains are a few crumbling sections of flint wall and a ruined gatehouse, a familiar but odd-looking sailor's landmark, because inside the gatehouse there stands the later ruin of a derelict mill tower. Some two hundred yards away, on slightly higher ground, stands a twenty foot high cross of Sandringham oak, presented by Queen Elizabeth in 1987 to mark the site of the High Altar. However, the Bishop of Norwich is still legally Prior of the Abbey and on the first Sunday in August sails from Horning to hold an annual service, which is popular with both locals and visitors.

The Abbey ruins are also visible from the top of the church tower of St. Mary's at Ranworth, but only just. There were almost 90 worn stone steps to climb up a narrow spiral staircase between flint-cobbled walls and then two ladders up to the final trapdoor opening on to the tower roof, but the views from the top were magnificent. Scanning the horizon through binoculars I counted twelve more church towers, a scattering of windmills, and far to the north the red and white tower of Happisburgh Lighthouse.

Far below were Ranworth and Malthouse Broad, two silver-grey circles in a figure of eight. Ranworth, to the left, was a silent and empty nature reserve. Malthouse was ringed with moored cruisers and sailboats, and while I watched the *Southern Comfort*, the Mississippi riverboat, appeared again. It made a slow and stately turnaround in Malthouse Broad, and then seemed to shrink and disappear up the narrow linking waterway between the nipped in waist between the two Broads and the main channel of the Bure.

In addition to those panoramic views, St. Mary's contains other treasures, a glorious painted mediaeval rood screen portraying the apostles and saints of the 15th century, and a beautiful illuminated Latin service book which originally came from Langley Abbey on the Yare. Ranworth itself is a comfortably spaced village of large thatched houses, a quayside pub called the *Maltsters* and, of course, the Staithe.

The Bure flows on to Acle, a pleasant little market town which has been called the Gateway to the Broads. In Saxon times Acle was actually a fishing village on the great estuary that was then the Bure. Now the river flows by half a mile to the north. Even more mercifully the constant flow of summer traffic, that once roared and snorted through the heart of the town on its way to Great Yarmouth and the coast, has also been diverted on to a new by-pass. When the by-pass was opened in 1989 thousands of local people celebrated with a street party, a carnival and a fete.

Acle has found peace once more and it is possible to appreciate the calm beauty of the lovely old church of St. Edmund, which stands on the corner as you turn into the main street. The church is again typical Norfolk, reed-thatched, with a Saxon round tower dating back before the Conquest, and an octagonal top added in the 13th century. The village green has a small monument to commemorate Queen Victoria's Jubilee, which also pinpoints its location, eleven miles from Norwich and eleven miles from Great Yarmouth, all carved in stone.

The river flows on to Stokesby, and the last safe moorings for boats before wending its way through a long, blue-veined jigsaw of green marshlands to where it joins with the Yare as they both exit through Great Yarmouth to the sea. There it is overlooked by the north-west tower, the last of the towers to be linked by the town's mediaeval walls. Here only a final 11 yards of wall was needed to take the defences right up to the river's edge.

The Bure is now a playground for visiting sailors, fishermen, walkers, bird-watchers, artists and a host of others who all find their pleasures on its waters or on its banks. But the Bure is also an ancient highway, its history woven by Romans and Saxons, raiding Vikings, monks and marshmen, keel boats and wherries. It is a river of haunting beauty, with a tale to tell at every bend and quayside.

FROM THE CITY TO THE SEA

11

11 FROM THE CITY TO THE SEA

The River Yare rises near the tiny village of Shipdham in central Norfolk, but for me it begins where it winds past Earlham Broad and those distinctive grey stone ziggurats of the University of East Anglia. The University has expanded with more new buildings since I studied there in the early eighties, but from the path that winds between the river and the lake it still looks pretty much the same. Bluebells carpet the woods nearby in spring, and the peaceful Yare footpath is the ideal place to wander while contemplating the lofty heights of pure philosophy.

THE ZIGGURATS OF UEA, REFLECTED IN THE CALM WATERS OF THE BROADS

The river skirts the southern environs of Norwich, the pride of Norfolk with its Norman castle, the cobbled mediaeval lanes of Elm Hill and the vast central market, a multi-coloured lake of striped awnings flanked by the magnificent flint Guildhall, all overlooked by the soaring brown brick clock tower of the Town Hall.

NORWICH CITY HALL
AND MARKET PLACE

For good measure there are two cathedrals, the City Cathedral, which like the castle we have already visited, and the great, squared stone edifice of St. John's Catholic Cathedral on

Earlham Road. There are also more than thirty splendid and mostly ancient churches gracing the city. One can only quote Sir John Betjeman on this aspect of ecclesiastical glory: "Remember Norwich! Round the corner, down the steps, up the Hill, over the bridge, there is always a church."

Norwich was founded in Saxon times as the village of Northwic, the first settlement on a gravel terrace above the Wensum. By 1004 it was a busy market centre, large enough to attract the attention of the marauding Danes. Despite being sacked and burned it continued to expand to fill the land between the Wensum and the Yare.

In the Middle Ages the Yare helped to make Norwich into the second greatest city in England. Most of the wool of East Anglia was shipped through its busy quaysides and down the river to the sea. Even before that glorious golden age, Norwich was rich and powerful enough to surround itself with more than four miles of massive flint boundary walls. Unfortunately this great avenue of sea-borne trade was something of a double-edged sword. Not only did it transport goods and wealth, the foreign ships from time to time brought in waves of plague and disease.

A few traces of the old city walls still remain, although the days of the great shipping merchants are gone. Until the 18th century Norwich was still one of the three most prosperous towns of England but the golden age of wool was over, and the new industrial revolution was favouring the booming steel and coal centres of northern England over agricultural Norfolk.

Times were changing. Norwich changed with them and became a leading centre in shoe-making. The river trade declined. Now tourism is a major factor and, where the Wensum meets the Yare, the river begins its new lease of life as a modern playground for holiday and pleasure craft. The city itself is a fascinating blend of the old and the new, with the magnificent Castle Mall shopping complex, all futuristic glass and escalators, contrasting with the narrow-lane maze of the ancient market.

The river leaves the city, passing under the modern road bypass that is the A47, and winding into its true heartland through a succession of wide-skied, flat marshes, each one a haven for hawks and wildfowl in winter, grazed by placid cows and sprinkled with wild flowers in summer. The villages here are mainly set back from the river, difficult for the stranger to find in the narrow, winding lanes.

NORFOLK
WHERRIES AT
ROCKLAND
ST. MARY

Bramerton Common is a hundred yards of neatly mown, perfect picnicking grass which slopes down to the edge of the river and 24 hour free moorings. When I saw it a sleek blue and white catamaran was the star of the handful of boats moored there. The little lane that eventually led me there was sign-posted to Woods End, which proved to be the large riverside pub a little further along.

You can walk the footpath down river to Surlingham, or find the lovely little flint church of St. Mary with its octagonal-topped round tower, where there is again room to park a car. From there I followed the church wall round to the path which circled the Surlingham Church Nature Reserve.

Where the way turned left across the marsh a few steep grassy steps to the right led up to the enigmatic ruins of St. Saviour's church, a few broken walls and window arches almost waist deep in long grass and thistles, the crumbled stonework strangled by grey and leafless ivy branches. Near this lonely but beautiful spot one of Norfolk's favourite characters, the naturalist Ted Ellis, lies buried.

The whole area is an RSPB reserve, a mixture of shallow pools, wet scrubland, dykes and marsh, managed as a haven and breeding ground for all sorts of birds and wildlife. Tall, yellow irises sprinkled the long grass with splashes of bright gold, and an almost missed sparkle of amber in the reeds proved to be a goldfinch, a beautiful little red, white and black-headed bird with golden-barred wings, which obligingly settled on a bare branch. It was obviously the wrong time of the year for the flocks of ducks, geese and hunting harriers which would later haunt these wetlands, and so the goldfinch was my bird-spotting highlight. The path wound back along a wide, looping S bend of the Yare and abruptly the church reappeared beyond a flint cottage through the trees.

The little village of Rockland St. Mary was originally named Rokelunda, because of its profusion of rooks. Because of its staithe which links it to the Yare, and the conveniently sited New Inn, it is still a popular mooring place for boats.

Here on a hot, August Sunday I found two of the last Norfolk wherries. Once these sleek and graceful, single sailed craft, with the high-pointed gaff rig, had been a common sight throughout all the broads rivers. Their unique design, including a removable keel, and a counter-balanced mast that could be dipped to pass under bridges, had been tailor-made for these often shallow and narrow waterways. For centuries, following on from the old square-rigged keel boats, they had carried goods and trade inland from the coast.

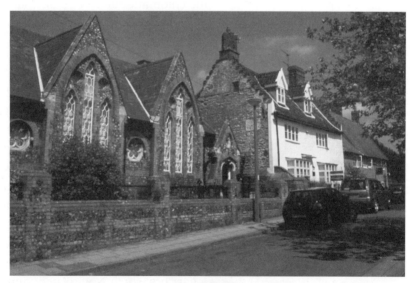

AT LODDON THE OLD FLINT LIBRARY OVERLOOKS
A QUIET AVENUE BY THE CHURCH GREEN

The traditional working boats have all but disappeared now but a few Edwardian built wherries still ply the tourist trade. Three are owned by the Wherry Yacht Charter and spend the summers giving sailing tours along the Bure and the Yare. The two at Rockland were welcoming visitors on one of their frequent open days.

Below Rockland the Yare passes Langley, a scattered village of farms and cottages, once famous for its great Abbey. The abbey church is long gone and the only comparable landmark now are the modern white towers of the Cantley sugar refinery, on the north side of the river.

Next comes the junction of the little River Chet, which feeds in from the south. The headwaters at Loddon were once a busy turning point for the wherries, overlooked by a 400 year-old white wood water mill, and today the little staithe is still flanked with boatyards and busy with modern pleasure cruisers, which stretch away as far as you can see around the disappearing bend of the river. The town itself is charming, brim-full of Georgian and Victorian architecture, with a lovely old flint school, now the library, facing the church green.

REEDHAM FERRY

Just below the Chet junction is Reedham, where the road stops at the edge of the river. The Yare is quite broad here, with a tide fall and rise of about three feet. A push on a bell button brings over the only ferryboat across the river. It's an old chain ferryboat, which cranks its way slowly and can take only three cars at a time. There is also an old iron railway swing bridge at Reedham, and then the Yare curls up into the Halvergate and Berney Arms marshes.

There are no roads here, and to visit the tall white-sailed, black tower landmark of the Berney Arms Mill you have to take the train from Reedham. It's a request stop, so if you want to get off you have to tell the conductor. The single rail track runs through flat mashes bisected by reed filled dykes. In high summer cows graze placidly, and black and white magpies flutter over lush green grassland dusted with yellow buttercups and purple clover. Old black windmill stumps are dotted all around the horizon, with smaller modern versions like a child's plastic windmill still lifting water from one dyke level to another.

Here the Yare opens out to enter Breydon Water, a single deep channel through wide mud and sand flats. The footpath along the bank is part of the Weaver's Way and looking across the river, up a slight slope of the far bank, were the long, solid walls of Burgh Castle. Once Roman soldiers would have walked those now ruined bastions, and their war galleys and trading ships would have filled a much wider and deeper version of Breydon Water.

If you have the energy you can walk the rest of the Weaver's Way all around the edge of the north flats and finish up at Britannia Pier on the seafront at Great Yarmouth. On the way you can see traces of the port's mediaeval past, two black flint towers from the 13th century town walls are still standing and at Greyfriars Cloisters you will find the remains of a Franciscan Friary from the same period.

YARMOUTH QUAY AND TOWN HALL

The Yare itself flows under the Haven swing bridge and on past the historic South Quay, once resplendent with the tall masts and the furled sails of the tall rigged ships. The annual maritime festival recreates those days, when flags and bunting fly over an armada of visiting vessels, both historic and modern. The festival can attract over 30,000 visitors, and the lusty sounds of the shanty men fill the air.

Once the famous Yarmouth Rows, 145 narrow cobbled lanes, some of them barely the width of a handcart, ran down to the river here, but most of them were destroyed by bombing in the Second World War. Fortunately the splendid Victorian and slightly Gothic Town Hall with its tall clock tower overlooking the quayside survived.

The Yare continues past the modern wharves on the opposite bank, where freighters still unload grain and timber. Yarmouth remains a busy port and still exploits its prime eastern seaboard position for direct trade with the ports of western Europe. The river passes behind the Golden Mile of yellow sand beaches with all the multi-coloured, light-flashing tourist attractions, amusement arcades and theatres and the long, fun-packed Wellington Pier. The seaside resort gives way to the long South Denes where the vast herring fleets once unloaded their silver harvest. Now there are caravan sites facing the sea, and facing the river all the support industries maintaining the oil and gas rigs exploiting the new riches offshore.

Here Nelson's monument, built in 1819 to commemorate Norfolk's hero, one of England's greatest sailors and the victor of the Battle of Trafalgar, towers over houses and factories, and the river mouth, where the Yare finally finishes its leisurely journey from the city to the cold North Sea.

CAPTION PLEASE

THE NORTH-WEST TOWER ON THE RIVERBANK,
ONCE THE FAR POINT OF THE OLD TOWN WALL

TAS VALLEY TALES

12

12 Tas Valley tales

The gentle Tas valley meanders south from Norwich, through an easy Norfolk landscape of farmlands and water meadows and church-proud villages, where square, round and octagonal flint towers nestle peacefully in leafy spots of woodland. You can speed through its heart, hurrying down the busy A140, and see nothing or take the time to make slow diversions on either side, and uncover some of Norfolk's hidden gems of rural tranquility and past history.

THE RIVER TAS
IS NOW A
WEED-CHOKED
STREAM, BUT
HERE THERE
WERE ONCE
BUSY
QUAYSIDES
SERVING THE
ANCIENT
ROMAN TOWN

There is evidence that the Tas valley has been inhabited to some extent for some 5,000 years and plainly it was once a much more important waterway than it is now. The land then was much wetter and the valley thick with oak forest before it was cleared. Before Norwich existed the Romans built *Venta Icenorum*, their main administrative town for central Norfolk on the Tas, the site is beside the modern village of Caistor St. Edmund, and close to where the river joins the Yare. Roughly a thousand years later the great Norman castle at Old Buckenham was built toward the head of the valley, the two great conquering invasions tenuously linked by the wandering river.

All that remains of *Venta Icenarum* today are the great, grassed earth embankments that once supported the town walls, now framing a large, open square field, empty except for the sheep which placidly graze the short grass, and the small, flint-towered parish church, which overlooks the site where the old Roman town once stood. It is easy to navigate the old town walls, a pleasant enough walk on a fine day, but now your own imagination has to fill in the ancient details.

The river that flows by is choked with rich green water plants, a stream that is narrowed in places to no more than a yard or two of clear water. But once it was a busy Roman waterfront with a wooden quayside where small riverboats loaded and off-loaded cargoes to and from the coast. The Tas was a source of water, enough to serve an estimated population of a thousand townspeople, with a bathhouse, two temples and a stone forum. It was also part of a Norfolk-wide transport network of waterways and a useful line of natural defence. It was clearly a deeper and more substantial flow then than it is now.

The name *Ventra Icenarum* translates as Market Place of the Iceni, which together with Iceni coins found here indicate that the site was previously a Celtic settlement. Because this whole area was once part of the tribal domain of the Iceni, a whole series of linked walks from Caistor to Diss along the eastern side of the valley has been designated as Boudica's Way, named to commemorate the Iceni Queen who challenged the might of Rome.

Along the western side of the valley is the Tas Valley Way, another series of linked walks. (Walking guides and leaflets for both routes are available from all Norfolk tourist information offices.) The two routes run roughly either side of the old Roman road to Colchester, which now, of course, is the A140. With a car you can pick and mix the highlights of the two as you wander south.

THE CHURCH OF ST. MARY AT SWARDESTON, WHERE
THE FATHER OF EDITH CAVELL WAS ONCE VICAR

Almost opposite Caistor, on the Tas Valley Way, is the delightful little village of Swardeston. Here we find another touch of history. The church of St. Mary The Virgin lies at the end of a leafy lane, hidden from the road by surrounding trees. You pass through an old wooden lichgate to enter the churchyard, and when I pushed open the heavy wooden door into the church itself I was met by the sweet smell of dahlias and lilies. The church was decorated for Harvest Festival.

It was almost too tranquil a setting for memories of the Second World War and the German firing squad which executed the British Nurse Edith Cavell for helping allied soldiers to escape from occupied Belgium. But this is the church where Edith Cavell worshipped and learned her childhood lessons in Sunday School. Her father was the Vicar here for fifty years, and now the east window is a stained glass memorial to the courage and sacrifice of Norfolk's heroine.

THE 16TH CENTURY BRIDGE OVER THE TAS AT NEWTON FLOTMAN

Just south of Swardeston is Mulbarton, no real history that I could discover, but worth a visit just to see it. The village is set round a huge open green, once 45 acres of common grazing, with charming cottages set around the duck pond, and the huge flint tower of its parish church framed by dark green yew trees and an elegant, almost small-town-America, white-painted picket fence.

At Newton Flotman, another long, sprawling village with a wide green and crowning church, there is a lovely old 16th century, three arch bridge across the river. It is beside the new bridge carrying the A140 and it is easy for most strangers to speed by without ever knowing that they have crossed the Tas.

Once there was a need for a ferryman here, the 'floteman' who gave the village its name.

A few miles downstream is Tasburgh and here we are back in history. There are more ancient earthworks here, and the information boards on the spot suggest that Tas is not a reference to the river but is probably derived from the name Tasa, while burgh is the old English word for a defended place or fort. The roughly oval site consists of an earthwork enclosure and a deep ditch, surrounded on three sides by the river and a side-stream.

Archaeological excavations in the area suggest that there were prehistoric settlements here between 9000 and 2000 BC, with most of the evidence dating from the Iron Age. The actual earthworks and the 900 year old round-tower church that stands just inside the boundary, date from the time of intensive Saxon settlement between AD 700 and 1200. Whether the defences were built by invading Vikings setting up a permanent camp, or by the native English hoping to withstand these violent marauders, is unknown.

ALCETON, WHERE ST.
GEORGE STANDS
OVER THE SLAIN
DRAGON ABOVE THE
PORCH OF ST.
MICHAEL'S

Still following the Tas Valley Way we find two more of those lovely old round tower Saxon churches for which Norfolk is renowned. Forncett St. Peter, in its charming wooded setting, is probably the most picturesque of the many churches along the way. St. Michael's at Alceton sits on a gentle hill, and above the door of the 18th century flint porch there stands a carved stone image of St. George with his feet firmly placed on top of a slain dragon.

The Tas now wanders in an eastward curve to Old and New Buckenham. The fact that there are two Buckenham's is due to William D'Albini, who decided to move the site of his Norman castle in

the middle of the 12th century. His existing castle at Old Buckenham he gave to Augustinian monks, who demolished it and
used the materials to construct themselves a priory, now also
gone. His new castle had probably the largest circular keep in
the country, of which only the lower storey, some twenty feet
high, now remains.

THE OLD MARKET CROSS, THE HEART OF NEW BUCKENHAM

The earth ramparts which once encircled the castle still remain,
rising in a thickly wooded hill from the placid, bramble-banked
surface of the old castle moat. The flint ruins of the keep nestle
in the hollow on the top of the hill. A locked gate stands across
the 15th century moat bridge, but the key can be obtained from
the garage on the opposite side of the main road. Once a
dominant symbol of Norman power and pride, Castle Hill is now

home only to wild birds, rabbits and butterflies. Autumn dresses it in brown and gold, summer in green and in spring daffodils grow in golden profusion beside the moat.

Both Buckingham's are themselves still thriving. New Buckenham is a perfect mediaeval town with streets lined by 15th to 17th century buildings, and the splendid perpendicular church of St. Martin's. In the centre of the village is the open Market Place, overlooked by an ancient Market House which was once a court and toll house. Part of the ground floor is open, the upper story supported by eight elegant Tuscan columns, and inside you can still find the central whipping post complete with arm clamps.

OLD BUCKENHAM,
THE OCTAGONAL
TOWER AND THE
THATCHED ROOF OF
ALL SAINT'S CHURCH

The Church of All Saints at Old Buckenham has almost all the elements of Norfolk's ecclesiastical rural charm. It has a completely octagonal tower, and a thatched nave and chancel roof over white-washed walls. The church is just slightly set back from one of the largest common greens in England, the land rights having been granted in mediaeval times. Old Buckenham also has a windmill, nothing unexceptional in Norfolk you might say, but this one has the largest diameter tower in England.

The Tas can in no way compete with the sea-bound holiday appeal of the larger rivers that run through the Norfolk Broads. There are no pleasure cruisers here, no wherries or yachts, no busy holiday centres. But if you seek a rest from all of that, some peaceful walking or cycling between some of the loveliest old churches in south Norfolk, then the Tas valley is tailor-made. Much of it is unpolluted and unspoiled, a seclusion of river valley meadows and green country lanes. Just try and avoid the awful A140.

WHERE ROMANS
MARCHED

13

13 WHERE ROMANS MARCHED

The disciplined, Eagle-bearing Legions who turned most of Europe and North Africa into the Roman Empire had a definite preference for marching in direct, arrow-straight lines. Roman roads, like the Empire itself, are famous for trampling over obstacles, rather than making detours or diversions. In west Norfolk they marched south to north in a slightly diagonal line that could almost have been drawn with a ruler, leaving a 46 mile path that we still know today as the Peddars Way, the name possibly derived from the Latin *Pedester*, or to go by foot.

The path begins at Knettishall Heath in Suffolk, a mixture of heath and woodland that leads down a pine and birch shaded, bracken-lined path to the gentle River Ouse, where a footbridge takes you over to Norfolk. Here the route of the Old Roman Road continues through more wild heathland and regimented forestry plantations, the haunt of roe deer and rabbits.

This is Breckland, land once cultivated but then allowed to revert to heath and woodland. The Anglo Saxons also grazed sheep and farmed rabbits here but the sparse soil is sand over chalk and the goodness in it was soon exhausted. Now the Forestry Commission has preserved the topsoil by planting rows upon rows of pine trees. There's another river to cross, the Thet at Brettenham, and then the path runs up to Wretham to skirt the edge of the Stanford Battle Area.

The villagers in this area were all dispossessed during the Second World War, to make way for an essential military training ground, and have never been allowed back. Now there is just a blank space on the map where the army play out their war games. I have been there several times, not as a soldier, but in my younger days as a retained firefighter. In the blistering hot summer of 1976, forest and heath fires were an everyday event and in the Battle Area we could be under fire in both senses of the word, when the racing flames found the occasional round of live ammunition that the soldiers had dropped.

AT WATTON, THE
TOWN SIGN
FEATURES THE
BABES IN THE WOOD

The small market town of Watton is on the site of an old Roman-British settlement that grew up beside the Roman road. It had its own Great Fire in the 1670s, and the clock tower in the High Street was built soon after to house a warning bell. The town sign commemorates the fairytale legend of the 'Babes in The Wood', who are supposed to have been found dead in nearby Wayland Wood.

The Way passes through the smaller village of Little Cressingham, which has a unique combined wind and water mill. To find the mill you go down the road signposted to Great Cressingham, passing the lovely old half ruined church of St. Michael. The church was partially restored in 1864 and the nave end of the building is still used in worship. However, the church tower has only two walls standing, with its roof open and blue sky and trees framed in the empty archways and windows. At the bottom of the hill is a stream and the mill.

A narrow channel of algae-green water leads up to the grey brick tower, white-railed at the half way mark but, at the time of writing, with no cap or sails. A little white pump house is built beside it containing a separate water wheel and a bramah pump, which once pumped water a mile away to Claremont Hall. The mill itself had two grinding stones on the ground floor which were turned by a water wheel, while two further pairs of stones in the upper half of the tower were wind driven by the sails. Trees shade the whole area now, and behind the mill a pair of swans were nesting where the water widened out.

The mill was built in 1821. It ceased working by wind power in 1916 but continued to work with water and oil power until 1952. The Norfolk Windmills Trust took over the mill in 1981, and are embarked upon an extensive programme of repairs and restoration. Eventually a new cap and sails are planned, and future walkers along the Peddars Way may divert to see it restored and fully operational.

From here The Way dips down into the shallow valley of the River Wissey between South and North Pickenham. The old Second Word War airfield here served briefly as a USAF bomber base, and from 1958 to 1963 was again in demand as a front-line Thor ICBM site in the stand-off Cold War. As in other sites across East Anglia, massive concrete launch pads were constructed for rockets with nuclear warheads on five minute stand-by, and not dismantled until 1963. Norfolk has not always been as peaceful and stress-free as it appears.

THE PEDLAR OF
SWAFFHAM

The Way passes by Swaffham, another lively market town, with its large triangular market dominated by the fine Butter Cross, looking like a small Greek temple with its Rotunda dome supported by eight columns. On top stands a statue of Ceres, the Roman Goddess of the Harvest. Behind it rises the tower and spire of the mediaeval church of Saints Peter and Paul, but overall in the background are the giant steel sails of the two towering modern wind turbines on the northern edge of the town. Both stand twice as high as Nelson's column, and one of them has a viewing platform that affords magnificent panoramic views over almost the whole of Norfolk.

At the north end of the market place stands a handsome town sign depicting a larger than life image of the Poor Pedlar of Swaffham. The story goes that the pedlar lived in Swaffham with his wife and family in a humble cottage beside a great oak tree. One night he had a strange dream. In the dream he learned that he would find his fame and fortune if he journeyed to far-off London and stood upon London Bridge. No doubt his good wife thought him drunk or daft, but off he went.

Having found his way to London Bridge he wandered up and down, wondering what to do next, and where on the bridge was his promised treasure. A bemused shopkeeper eventually gave way to his own curiosity, approached the pedlar and asked him what he was doing. The pedlar explained. The shopkeeper laughed out loud. "Last night I had a dream," he chuckled, "I went to a town in Norfolk and dug under a great oak tree, and there I found a pot of treasure. But I'm not daft enough to waste my time going there." The enlightened pedlar hurried home, dug under his own oak tree and found a pot filled with gold coins. Later he is said to have found an even greater fortune buried underneath the pot.

The name of the pedlar is recorded as John Chapman and, among the list of names of those who have paid notable donations to the church of St. Peter and St. Paul, the name of John Chapman appears as the man who paid for the North Aisle. This John Chapman was a church warden who had his own family pew. So perhaps there was a pedlar who came into a fortune and felt the need to give thanks. You may draw your own conclusions.

Before the Romans came this was the land of the Iceni, and to get a glimpse of how these ancient Britons lived it is worth the three and a half mile diversion to the south-east to find Cockley Cley, where one of their villages has been re-created on its original site. There is a moat and a palisade, and inside a village of reed-thatched buildings. What you see is what probably existed before the Romans razed it to the ground as part of the ferocious reprisals for Boudicca's bloody rebellion.

Carry on to Castle Acre, where the Peddars Way crosses the little River Nar by a small bridge beside the ancient ford, and you have moved into the Middle Ages. Already you can see glimpses of the splendid ruins of the vast Cluniac Priory built by the Norman overlord, William de Warenne. On the far side of the valley the road climbs up to pass through the massive Bailey Gateway into the village with its charming tree-shaded green flanked by brick and flint cottages. To the right are the grass-humped remains of the castle that give the village its name, and to the left the road leads to the priory.

Here the Peddars Way is crossed by the Green Way, the ancient pilgrim route which ran from Ely to the Shrine of Our Lady at Walsingham. The priory was a much appreciated resting place for the hundreds of thousands of ordinary pilgrims who made the journey before the Dissolution, and for twelve out of a line of thirteen English Kings. Even Henry VIII made the Royal pilgrimage to Walsingham just five months before he closed down both the priory and the shrine. The two ancient track ways ran together briefly from Swaffham to Castle Acre, and then the Green Way separated again and ran north east through West Lexham and Fakenham to Walsingham.

The Peddars Way continues almost due north, passing close by Great and Little Massingham, which must be two of the prettiest villages along The Way. At Great Massingham the flint tower of St. Mary's Church overlooks two small lakes and a spacious, neatly mown village green. The lakes are both filled with floating mallard and flanked by clumps of tall rushes, fishermen, and 18th and 19th century cottages, in roughly that order.

THE PLACID CALM OF GREAT MASSINGHAM

Still heading north the Way passes between the great palladian mansion of Houghton Hall about two miles to the east, and the Queen's residence at Sandringham about four miles to the west. Also to the east, as the trail pushes on, you can see in the distance the five storey, black-tarred Bircham's Windmill with its white cap and sails. It's the only restored and working windmill in the area and on a breezy day the sails may well be turning.

At Bircham Heath four funerary barrows have been excavated to reveal Bronze Age finds and this whole area, slashed by The Way between Bircham, Snettisham and Ringstead, has yielded hundreds of Bronze Age torcs, the heavy twisted necklets of gold or silver wire that were worn by Celtic nobles and their ladies as symbols of their wealth. One major hoard found at Snettisham is the largest cache of gold and silver treasure ever found in Britain.

HOUGHTON HALL, A PALLADIAN MANSION

The Peddar's Way ends at Holme Next the Sea, where magnificent long-grassed dunes roll down to the sandy beach under those magnificent high Norfolk skies. Not far from here another ancient site of uncertain significance was recently uncovered by the shifting pattern of the sea and tides. A circle of sea-blackened timbers was revealed with what could have been an oak altar stump in the centre, which was promptly christened Sea Henge. It was possibly 4,000 years-old, and its possible original purpose, a site of mysterious Druidic rites or ancient Celtic sun or moon worship, were the fantasy ingredients of unbridled speculation. The archeologists took it all away for further study and now the wild, gull-flown sand dunes are as empty and lonely as before.

THE REMAINS OF ST. EDMUND'S CHAPEL FRAME
THE OLD LIGHTHOUSE AT OLD HUNSTANTON

To find some human habitation you have to turn left for Hunstanton, Norfolk's prime holiday spot on this corner where the coast turns into The Wash. The new town of fun fairs, green esplanades and red brown cliffs is better known but first you will come to Old Hunstanton, the original fishing village. Here the young Saxon Prince Edmund was shipwrecked in AD 855, when a violent storm overtook his ship on his journey from his

German homeland. The ruins of the chapel, built later by the monks of Bury St. Edmunds in thanksgiving for his survival, still remain on a cliff top near the 18th century lighthouse. Presumably, after his deliverance, Edmund then used the Peddar's Way to continue his journey to destiny and martyrdom as the new Christian King of East Anglia.

Today all that is left of the chapel are the foundations and one standing, buttressed archway. In 1918 a Garden of Rest was created here to commemorate the local men who died in the First World War, and in summer it is filled with red roses and purple lavender.

It is worth finding your way down to the beach, just to stroll along the base of those spectacular cliffs. The three different coloured rock layers are made up of carstone, red chalk and white chalk. Once there was a prehistoric sea here, before the land mass of East Anglia was formed, and fossils found in the chalk tell us that it was alive with the ancestors of today's cuttlefish and squid. Later huge earth movements lifted up the land to form what is now Norfolk, and in those early days the surrounding sea was warm and tropical, and the climate probably similar to the Caribbean today. Hunstanton's Leisure and Tourism Department promotes the town, sometimes optimistically, as "Sunny Hunny." In those days it almost certainly was.

Alternatively, as you reach Holme and the sea, you can go right to find pretty little Thornham, where there are wooden jetties and moored fishing boats along the creeks between the salt marsh and the mud flats, and best of all, a comfortable pub. You have now left the Peddar's Way and are heading along the equally well-marked and well-trodden Norfolk Coast Path, but that's another story.

BIRCHAM WINDMILL, FULLY RESTORED AND STILL GRINDING CORN

STATELY HALLS

14

14 STATELY HALLS

Norfolk was once a county composed almost entirely of great country estates, dominated by the land-owning gentry. The prominent land-owners during the Middle Ages were the church, the religious orders and the monasteries, building their wealth from the vast flocks of sheep that grazed the gentle hills and summer meadows.

By Tudor times fortunes were also being made from the legal profession and from successful careers at court, and much of this new money was also buying its way into the elite and refined world of country gentlemen. These men were well poised to take advantage of the Dissolution when almost all the vast monastic lands came up for grabs.

Three centuries later agriculture had mainly replaced sheep. Turnip Townsend had become famous for his agricultural innovations at Raynham, and it was bankers and businessmen who were buying their way into the ranks of the landed gentry. Deer parks and managed woodland for the great pheasant shooting parties, and the entertainment of royalty, had become the order of the day.

At the centre of every great estate was the great house, the stately home or the magnificent hall. The architectural historian George Winkley, in his *Country Houses of Norfolk,* has listed more than sixty of these splendid homes which still remain scattered across the county. They range over every architectural style, from moated Tudor mansions, through glorious gothic piles and luxurious Jacobean or Italianite palaces, to the great Palladian houses which in part resemble Greek or Roman temples. Most of them are still private homes but half a dozen of the mightiest and the best, some of them under the care of the National Trust, are now major tourist attractions and are open to all.

The oldest of these is Oxburgh Hall, with its echoes of a mediaeval castle in the great moat and the magnificent red brick towered gateway with crenellated battlements. On a fine summer's day the lovely old brickwork glows almost orange in the sunlight, and is reflected back in the still waters of the moat. The gatehouse was built in 1482 and, after Caister Castle, is one of the oldest brick-built homes in the county. There is almost no natural stone in Norfolk, so prior to the advent of brickmaking, even the most solid structures were mainly of wood or flint.

OXBURGH HALL AND MOAT FROM THE SOUTH AND EAST

Oxburgh was built during turbulent times, the Wars of the Roses were raging, and many of the nobility lost their lives or their fortunes through supporting the wrong side. Sir Edmund Bedingfield who built Oxburgh received his royal permission from Edward of York. However, he was fortunately not present at Bosworth Field when the crown finally passed to the House of Lancaster. He did later fight for the new King Henry VII at Stoke in 1487 to see off a last ditch Yorkist challenge, and so successfully switched loyalties. The Bedingfield family has consistently held on to Oxburgh ever since.

THE JACOBEAN ELEGANCE OF BLICKLING HALL

Oxburgh is in the south-west corner of the county, not far from Swaffham, move up to the north east, just past Aylsham, and you will find what has to be one of the most magnificent sights in Norfolk. A sudden bend in the road after passing through concealing woodlands, and you are abruptly confronted with the vast gravel drive sweeping up to Blickling Hall. On either side are neatly manicured green lawns and two high yew hedges, then the tall-chimneyed, dutch-gabled, red-brick office and old stable blocks, all forming the perfect approach to this splendid Jacobean mansion of high turrets and towers.

Finding something to lead the eye into the essence of the picture, is one of the golden rules in all the photography manuals I have ever read, and that makes Blickling a photographer's dream.

Blickling Hall was built by Sir Henry Hobart in 1619. He had to pull down an old moated manor house that had once been owned by the Boleyn family, and it is said that the ghost of the ill-fated Ann Boleyn occasionally drives an equally ghostly carriage through the grounds. The park estate is vast, 4,777 acres, which takes in woodlands, a lake and 25 farms. It stretches along the bank of the River Bure, and includes a small, classic Doric temple built by the First Earl of Buckinghamshire in 1730. The extensive gardens are a joy to explore in any season.

FELBRIGG HALL, THE SOUTH AND EAST CORNER

Another superb, 17th century house, built at the same time as Blickling and even employing some of the same craftsmen and the same architect, is Fellbrigg Hall, nearer to the coast and only three miles from Cromer. Here the massive south front is dominated by projecting bay windows and a central square porch tower, and all across the front runs stone balustrading which proclaims the words 'Gloria Deo In Excelsis' – Glory to God in The Highest.

The new, red-brick west front was not built until the mid 1680s and provides a smart, modern contrast to the mellow stone bays and porch of the old front. From the south-west it almost looks as though two separate houses are standing corner to corner. Such is the speed with which building styles could change.

Holkham, built on the north Norfolk coast a century later, separated from the vast sweep of the beach and the sea by a belt of pine trees and sand dunes, is a complete contrast again. It was inspired by the Grand Tour of Europe, which all country gentlemen were then in the habit of taking to complete their classical education. A majestic Palladian mansion built of yellow brick on a star pattern with a central block and four corner pavilions, it has a magnificent south-facing porch modeled on the Parthenon. The porch overlooks a large circular fountain where St. George is permanently poised in the act of slaying the dragon, under curving sprays of water splashing from the upturned mouths of swans and fishes.

The magnificent, columned marble hall where visitors enter on the north side is modelled on a Roman temple. It leads on to staterooms containing one of the greatest assemblies of treasures and antiquities ever to have been brought home from Europe, for Holkham was not only inspired in style by the Grand Tour, it was also built to house all that young Thomas Coke had collected in his extended travels.

ST. GEORGE PERMANENTLY SLAYING THE DRAGON IN THE
SPECTACULAR FOUNTAIN IN FRONT OF HOLKHAM HALL

In a similar vein is Houghton Hall, where the central block is
connected to two-storeyed wings by curving colonnades,
another Palladian masterpiece built in the 1720s by Sir Robert
Walpole, the First Prime Minister of Great Britain. Four majestic
cupola domes rise above the four corners of the central block,
and the west front has a huge, zig-zag double staircase ascending
to meet four lofty Doric columns supporting an elaborate triangular gable. Above the gable stand three life-size statues of
Demosthenes, the Defender of Liberty, Minerva, the Goddess
of Wisdom, and Justice with her sword and scales.

Like Holkham, Houghton is surrounded by rolling parkland, a
six mile walk around the perimeter, with free-roaming herds
of white fallow deer. Proud peacocks also wander the lawns with

outspread tails. In the stable block there is a hidden delight for the small boy at the heart of every man, a magnificent toy soldier collection with a detailed tableau of almost every major battle in British military history.

Almost everywhere you go at Houghton you will see representations of the Saracen's Head crest, said to have been granted in 1191 to a Crusader Walpole who fought at the great siege of Acre. The Walpoles built and owned Houghton until 1797, when the house passed to the Cholmondleys. The present owner is the Seventh Marquess of Cholmondley.

The third great house in north-west Norfolk is Sandringham. The house and grounds belong to Her Majesty, The Queen, and the vast estate includes seven villages and a large number of tenant farms. Four generations of English monarchs have found rest and relaxation here since it was purchased in 1862 for the young Edward VII and his future Queen Alexandra.

There had been a house on the site for centuries but Edward and Alexandra had most of it pulled down and then rebuilt to create the wonderful arrangement of house, lakes and gardens, all nestling in the glorious park and woodlands which we see today.

During the early 19th century the great aristocratic sport of pheasant shooting was at its height on all these estates and up to 28,000 birds each season were being shot at Sandringham alone. In the old royal stables there is now a museum containing some of the old shooting brakes and faded black and white photographs which bring back those past, crisp autumn days, when the sporting guns would line up to meet the birds as they were flushed up and over their heads by the advancing lines of game-keepers and beaters. Another glimpse of the gentry at play in their hey-day.

THE SPLENDID TOWERS OF SANDRINGHAM RISING ABOVE
THE LAKES AND WOODLAND OF SANDRINGHAM PARK

There has been no space here to describe the sumptuous interiors of these magnificent stately homes: the luxurious staterooms, the marbled corridors, stairways and halls, the incredibly intricate plasterwork ceilings; their furnishings, the paintings, the statuary, the tapestries and the treasures. All of this simply has to be seen.

No space either to detail all the fascinating stories of the great families who built them and have lived in them, their Lords and Ladies, the Knights and Squires, the Barons, Dukes and Earls, as they have moved in and out of the power games of English history.

The few houses mentioned here are but the tip of an iceberg; the majority of Norfolk's remaining stately halls and manor houses are still privately owned, set back from the main roads and screened by woodlands. So make the most of these that are on public view. The full appreciation of all these beautiful houses and all they have to offer is a learning experience best enjoyed on the spot. Visit them and you will not be disappointed.

SANDRINGHAM –
A ROYAL FLOWER SHOW

15

15 SANDRINGHAM –
A ROYAL FLOWER SHOW

We cannot take our leave of Norfolk's stately halls, and particularly of Sandringham, without mentioning the Sandringham Flower Show. Officially, of course, it's the Sandringham Estate Cottage Horticultural Society Trust Flower Show, and has been held annually for more than 120 years at Sandringham Park adjoining the magnificent Royal Residence of Sandringham House. Until her sad death in 2002 Her Majesty The Queen Mother was a patron of the show and over the years, due to her regular personal attendance and her obvious deep affection for the show, it had become an event that she had made uniquely her own.

A HORSE DRAWN CARRIAGE CONVEYED THE QUEEN MOTHER
AND PRINCE CHARLES TO AND FROM THE SHOW

I was fortunate enough to visit the show in 2001, the last year the Queen Mother was able to attend, and later interviewed Show Chairman David Reeve for a feature in the Norfolk Journal.

"She always arrives promptly at eleven o'clock," David told me with open admiration. "Never a minute after nor a minute before. She arrives in an open horse-drawn carriage, and she is on the showground for approximately an hour and a half. In recent years, now that she has passed her hundredth birthday, she has used her electric buggy to get around the show, but her commitment to the show and her determination to meet and talk to all the people she meets every year has never wavered. Over the years we have not varied the route with any short cuts, nor omitted any of her traditional stops, and of course, we would not do so unless we were requested to do so."

He smiled as he added, "I don't know how she does it but I've never known her to attend a wet show. I've seen it rain before she arrives, and I've seen it rain after she's left, but somehow she always seems to bring with her the sunshine."

I had met with David at his home in Dersingham, one of several parishes which make up the Sandringham estate. David is an ex Police Chief Superintendent and for ten years was head of the Royal Protection Unit at Sandringham. "It was a rewarding job and a huge privilege," he recalled. "When you join the police you take an allegiance to the Queen, but you never actually expect that you will have the honour to meet her and to work directly for her. The job also meant that I was invited to sit upon the committee for the Flower Show, because it is important that you do integrate with the Sandringham community. When I retired from the Police Force I was elected Chairman of the Flower Show committee, so I was fortunate in being able to continue my association with Sandringham, and with the Royal Family and the Flower Show."

THE QUEEN MOTHER'S LAST APPEARANCE
AT THE SANDRINGHAM FLOWER SHOW

"In recent years we've also been fortunate in that the Prince of Wales attends with the Queen Mother," David continued. "Prince Charles is also an enthusiastic gardener and he takes a keen interest in all aspects of the show. However, I don't think he would mind me saying that he always puts a little distance between himself and The Queen Mother, possibly because like all the rest of us he too sees it as her show. He's a very popular Royal in his own right but he always generates that little gap as if to give his Grandmother the prime position."

I knew exactly what he meant. During the show David had found me a place in the press pen where I was focussing my camera entirely on the Queen Mother as she approached the flower marquee in her buggy. Every foot of the way she stopped to shake a few more hands and receive a few more bouquets from the enthusiastic crowds that lined her route. Prince Charles was a discreet distance back, shaking hands and greeting people on the sideline, and I almost missed him until he was only a few feet away.

To the general public the Sandringham Flower Show is an annual one-day event which always takes place on the last Wednesday in July, but in fact the Show is the culmination of two important competitions which involve the competitors in preparing their gardens throughout the year. The first is for the well established King George VI Cup, and the second for the more recently introduced Queen Mother's Cup.

HAPPY FAMILIES
RELAXING IN FRONT
OF SANDRINGHAM
CHURCH

Flowers and produce from the estate gardens are exhibited and judged on the day, but the gardens themselves are judged beforehand. The King George Cup was established to encourage the cottagers and householders on the estate to raise and maintain the standards of their gardens, and the judging inspection looks to a whole range of qualifying categories, including flowers, vegetables and fruit trees. Points are awarded in each category and a garden has to make a good score in all categories in order to carry off the trophy.

"It is a very strict competition," David explained, "with very precise rules. The King George Cup competition has been a huge success for many years, but because the ways in which people maintain their gardens have changed we have now introduced the Queen Mother Cup to run alongside it. Most people no longer grow vegetables and fruit trees because sadly it is so much easier to go and buy this produce in the supermarkets. Also modern couples tend to lead more busy lives, and their gardens reflect this, by being designed to need less maintenance and with more emphasis on patios and lawns."

"So we introduced the Queen Mother Cup, which quite simply has virtually no rules. This is something we agreed with Her Majesty, and this competition has also proved to be a huge success. The only guidance we give the judges is that the garden has to be pleasing to the eye, so that really encompasses everything. It could be lawns and shrubs, it could be a patio garden, it could be a Mediterranean or a Japanese garden, or any modern style of garden that you can think of. There are no limitations and that is a quite refreshing new approach."

The cup competitions are only open to people living in the parishes on the estate, and the same applies to the Cottagers' Classes of arranged vegetables, fruit and flowers, and bakery and preserves that are exhibited and judged on the day. But the show also has Open Amateur Classes and these can attract entries from anywhere in the country. A walk through the flower marquee is a walk through a floral wonderland of fragrance and colour, of magnificent cut roses, phlox, carnations, dahlias, gladioli, lilies and almost every flower you can imagine.

"The Committee gave a lot of thought to the introduction of the Queen Mother's new cup," David assured me. "Because change is something which we are very careful about. We already have a very successful show so we do not believe in change for the sake of change. We've also introduced a new Horticultural Exhibitors Marquee, which is an exhibition marquee for a number of countrywide specialist growers. We have one exhibitor who specializes in roses, another in clematis, and another in conifers and alpines, and that too has proved hugely successful."

MIXED VEGETABLES EXHIBITED IN THE COTTAGERS CLASSES

Generally, though, our show is so successful that all we feel we really need to do is tinker around the edges from time to time, just to make sure that it is all running smoothly. We have people who have been coming to the Sandringham Flower Show for fifty or sixty years, they have brought their children and they now bring their grandchildren. Usually we only make subtle changes, like varying the entertainments events. We like to have an aerial display. Last year it was the Spitfire Tigers Freefall Display Team and this year we have the Firebird Aerobatic Team. Last year we had the Essex Police Band and the Lake Wobegon Brass Band from the USA, and this year we've got the Band of The Dragoon Guards and the Springwood High School Band. So there's a similarity to the attractions but the actual formulae of the show remains the same."

The formulae clearly works, for the show regularly pulls visitor numbers in excess of 15,000 and has raised more than a quarter of a million pounds for charity. And that is without including the amounts which the charity stalls raise for themselves.

It is a wonderfully traditional show and one of its regular features is a cricket match between the Sandringham Eleven and the Royal Warrant Holders. It is a gloriously, shamelessly, high summer British event, rich in the scent of flower blossoms and the sound of willow smacking leather. The huge crowds stroll, laugh and play against the splendid background of white marquees, rows of colourful trade and charity stalls, and the flint tower of Sandringham church standing tall against a July blue sky.

It is all very Heart of England, with the warm, happy atmosphere of a small village fete where nearly everybody knows nearly everybody else and they have all been coming for years. There are hundreds of small village fetes and garden shows throughout Norfolk in the summer which share that small community warmth and familiarity, which has at Sandringham spread through a truly mammoth show.

THEIR LAST SHOW TOGETHER, BUT PRINCE CHARLES
CONTINUES TO PROVIDE ROYAL SUPPORT

Of course, that is why it is truly unique, because it is held at Sandringham, where the support of the Royal Family for the show is only equaled by the joyful support of the crowds for the Royal Family. Since the Queen Mother passed away Prince Charles has come into the foreground and continues to regularly support the show with a personal appearance. His visits mean that Sandringham continues to be a very Royal Flower Show.

THE SHOWGROUND BLENDS THE ATMOSPHERE OF A FRIENDLY VILLAGE FETE
WITH ALL THE ATTRACTIONS OF A TRULY MAMMOTH SHOW

Dancing in the May

16

16 DANCING IN THE MAY

The origins of May Day celebrations go back to Roman times and beyond, some of the deeper roots disappearing into the mists of Celtic and Pagan mythology. They are bound up with fertility rites and welcoming in a new season of growth, re-creation and light. Dancing the dawn up to welcome the First Day of May, gathering flowers and fresh green garlands all play their part.

THE KING'S MORRIS
PERFORM ONE OF
THEIR COTSWOLD
DANCES

The pre-Christian Roman link goes back to Flora, the Goddess of Flowers. The original Flora was a celebrated courtesan, who bequeathed her fortune to the people of Rome to provide for an annual celebration of her memory which would include singing, dancing and drinking. By all accounts her festival, the *Floralia*, soon became a happy and licentious affair, in which Flora was always represented as a beautiful maiden wearing a crown of flowers. Soon after she became deified as a Goddess she became the Goddess of Flowers and Springtime, which firmly associated her with May Day. In modern scientific language her name has also come to embrace all of flower and plant life.

When the Romans invaded Britain they brought all their beliefs, customs and festivals with them. One colony settled on the soggy marshes of West Norfolk at what is now King's Lynn, and it is possible that they introduced the Romanized version of their May Day celebrations into the area. Two millennia later the May Day Garland, with Flora represented by a doll seated within two hoops of flowers and greenery, is again carried in an exuberant procession around the modern streets of the town.

The Merrie England picture of the Middle Ages centres around the May Day image of young maids and gallants dancing around the maypole. Many English towns had permanent maypoles, and there are two such references in a *History of Lynn* published in 1812. In 1682 two maypoles were recorded as being set up in the town, one in the Tuesday Market Place and the other at St. Ann's fort. And in 1685 the market place maypole is recorded as being taken down to be replaced by the King's statue.

Maypole dancing and May Garlands are separate traditions, although both involved getting up early on the May morning to gather flowers and greenery from the fields and woodlands. Some early accounts suggest that young men and maids would pair off to spend the night in the woods, engaged in 'pleasant pastimes', to reappear in the May dawn with a young tree and sprays of green to set up in the town or village as the focus for dancing. In King's Lynn, however, by the 19th century at least, the May Garland tradition had become one that was almost wholly carried out by children.

The boys and girls of Lynn would get up early to throw open their doors and greet the May Day, and their first task would be to run out and gather the flowers and green sprays they needed for their garlands. The height of their naughtiness was to nail up the door latches of any sleepy-headed friends who had lingered too long in bed. The garlands they made consisted of two large hoops, each covered with alternate twists of flower blossoms and greenery. The doll representing Flora would be set in the centre, and the whole thing finished off with coloured ribbons and strings of blown bird's eggs.

Then, throughout the day, these garlands would be mounted on a pole and carried about the town by the different groups of children. All of them would be blowing lustily on cow horns and ox horns to announce their presence, and, of course, the main aim would be to collect a few pennies in appreciation of their musical antics.

The most famous image of all this is taken from *Hone's Table Book of 1828*, a copy of which is still held in the King's Lynn Museum. It shows a procession group from the St. James Workhouse, carrying their May Garland through the streets. The oldest resident of the workhouse carried the garland but his accompanying troupe of prancing horn-blowers are all pauper children in the dark blue parish livery.

The workhouse garland was the largest one in use and it was carried about the town annually until 1836. The town's corporation had officially prohibited the event a year earlier, presumably because the noise and the begging element was deemed to constitute a public nuisance. However, other May Garlands were still being carried around King's Lynn until 1914, at least, and possibly as late as the 1930s, although the horn-blowing seems to have disappeared in the late 19th century.

May Garlands were not unique to King's Lynn. Peterborough and Northampton were among other towns which had such a tradition, and it was also kept alive in the villages of Shouldham and West Winch just to the south-east of King's Lynn. In Lynn the school registers in the 19th century regularly contained comments about many children being absent to partake in May Day, but in the villages it was more a case of 'if you can't beat them, join them'. The schoolrooms there were described as elegantly decked with flowers for the occasions, and lists were kept of each year's May Queen and King. In Shouldham the tradition was kept up at least until Edwardian times and the flowers were usually supplied from the gardens of the local squire.

THE KING'S MORRIS IN FULL SWING

I learned all of this from David Jackson, the bagman of The King's Morris, the Morris Men of King's Lynn, who have revived and refurbished this wonderful ancient tradition, and have again made the King's Lynn May Garland Procession into an eagerly awaited annual event.

THE MAY GARLAND IN PROCESSION THROUGH THE STREETS OF KING'S LYNN

"The King's Morris was formed in 1978," David told me. "And from 1980 onwards we have always celebrated May Day by Dancing the Dawn up. We go up to the top of Knights' Hill, which is the highest point near King's Lynn. We're there by five a.m. and there perform the traditional Morris ritual of dancing as the sun rises. Then in 1983 we revived the tradition of the King's

Lynn May Garland. They are separate traditions but together they now make up our annual May Day celebrations."

After Dancing the Dawn up, The King's Morris usually resort to their rehearsal hall for a full English breakfast to set themselves up for the rest of the day. By twelve noon they will be at the Saturday Market Place between the splendid twin towers of 12th century St. Margaret's church and the flint chequer-board facade of the 15th century Guildhall of The Holy Trinity, there to begin their next Morris dancing display.

This was where I found them on May Day, performing an energetic set of Cotswold Morris dances in their uniform of white shirts and trousers and grey top hats, and their ribbons of blue and yellow, the colours of the King's Lynn heraldic shield. Eventually they moved off to march in procession up the High Street, proudly holding aloft the magnificent green and flower-decked May Garland. In keeping with tradition most of them were blasting away with their curved cows horns. They circled the town centre, stopping wherever there was sufficient room to dance and again entertain the following crowd.

I had noticed that there were at least two classes of schoolchildren present with their teachers, and David explained:

"Because it had become so much a children's tradition before it died out, we do now try to keep the essence of that alive. We want the children to be aware of their local folk culture, and so we encourage the schoolchildren to come along and whenever possible join us in the procession. We have supplied the schools with details of the tradition and its history, and with frameworks so that pupils can make their own May garlands."

"Part of the old tradition was that each children's group would end the day by suspending their own garland across the street, and then play a game of handball where the garland was used as a target. That's one aspect which we couldn't resurrect, but we do try to involve the children as much as possible. Another difference, of course, is that Morris dancing was never a part of the original tradition, but because we are Morris dancers we've added in our own displays. We try to make it a day of good, all round entertainment, as well as keeping the spirit of May Day alive."

"We always hold the May Garland procession on the actual day," David said in conclusion. "If it happens to be a working day then that can cause some problems in getting all the dancers together. We usually have some help from the members of Peterborough Morris to make our numbers up. But when May Day falls on a Saturday we'll be there in full strength, and we can usually count on a few more Morris sides to make it a really good event. Then we usually keep the dancing going all through the afternoon."

BLOWING UP A
MAY DAY STORM

NORFOLK SHOWTIME

17

17 NORFOLK SHOWTIME

The King's Morris are not the only Morris side dancing in Norfolk, and May Day is not the only day on which you will find them in full swing. May Day is only the start of the summer season and every year throughout June, July and August you can see Morris dancers performing throughout the length and breadth of the county. They are part of our glorious English heritage, dancing outside pubs, on village greens and in town centres, and always a colourful spectacle in their flamboyant costumes. With feet flying, bells jangling, sticks thwacking or handkerchiefs waving, they are a lively free folk show, best enjoyed while savouring a pint of good Norfolk ale.

One of the best known sides is Kemp's Men, who take their name from Will Kemp, one of the key inspirations of Morris folklore. The millennium year 2000 saw the celebration of the 400th anniversary of that acknowledged hero's most famous achievement, for in the year 1600 the Great Will Kemp danced all the way from London to Norwich to win a series of wagers. All through East Anglia Morris Dancers celebrated a re-creation of that event, which has become known as Kemp's *NINE DAIES WONDER!*

Will Kemp was a contemporary of Shakespeare, a dancing actor-cum-clown who was the original Dogberry in *Much Ado About Nothing*. He was one of Lord Chamberlain's Men and was much-loved for his ribald verse and song. However, his popularity with the common crowd proved his downfall when his troupe moved to the new Globe Theatre in 1599. The up-market nature of the new venue meant that Kemp's rude vulgarity was out-of-place, and so he had to leave.

Out of work and in debt he set out to re-coup his fortunes with his multiple wager. He laid a number of bets at three to one in his favour that he would dance all the way from London to Norwich in the nine days prescribed by the wager, with no more than the set rest days the wager allowed.

Despite foul roads and fouler weather he won his bet, and his place in Morris dancing history.

THE SCROLL OF GREETING, CARRIED FROM THE LORD MAYOR OF LONDON TO THE MAYOR OF NORWICH

Kemp danced with one drummer, one servant and an overseer to ensure that he kept to the terms of the wager. On April 15th 2000 six dancers, two musicians on melodium and recorder, and their support team, all set out from London's Royal Exchange to re-enact the *Nine Daies Wonder*. Since AD 1600 times have changed and so have the roads, but their aim was to keep as closely as possible to Kemp's original route. Like Kemp they carried with them a scroll of greetings from the Lord Mayor of London to the Lord Mayor of Norwich.

In addition to the full distance team who were dancing the entire route they were met, entertained and escorted by local Morris sides through all the counties of Essex, Suffolk and Norfolk. It was a full week of Morris Magic, with practically every Morris dancer and his brother participating in one way or another.

I met up with them on the fifth day of their epic dance. They had been averaging three miles an hour and eighteen miles a day since leaving London, and were still leaping and waving as cheerfully as ever. They had passed through the pain barrier on the second day, one of the dancers told me, and now they were ignoring their aches and blisters.

I read later in *The East Anglian Daily Times*, that the dancers had finally reached Norwich on the Saturday, dancing in triumph through the city streets to hand over that all important scroll from one mayor to the other. One of the dancers had carried it rolled up in a blue metal tube strapped to the back of his waist for the whole 127 miles.

Will Kemp had taken sixteen days in all, his nine daies a-dancing, plus all seven of his allowed rest days. The modern Morris men had not only danced the route without any rest days, but had clipped a day off Will Kemp's nine and completed it in eight! They were footsore and weary. They had gained blisters and lost toenails, but they too had won their hard-earned place in Morris dancing history.

RE-CREATING WILL KEMP'S NINE DAY WONDER

Today the spirit of Will Kemp is still very much alive and flour-ishing in Norfolk, with Kemp's Men and all the other Morris sides. A good time to see them all en masse is at the annual Potty Morris Festival in Sherringham, organized by the town's Potty Morris Dance Side.

There are many other regular summer events which should simply not be missed. In complete contrast to the high-stepping, fast stomping Morris dancers is the annual World Snail Racing Championship held every year at Congham near King's Lynn. Newmarket may be the horse-racing capital of the world and Le Mans may be the top venue for motor racing, but for snail racing, world championship class, you have to come to West Norfolk and Congham.

AT THE ANNUAL CONGHAM WORLD SNAIL RACING CHAMPIONSHIP,
READY, STEADY, SLOW! AND THEY'RE OFF

Congham is next door to Grimston and the snail racing is all part of the annual Congham village fete, which is actually held on Grimston cricket pitch, but as Grimston cricket pitch is actually in Congham that's just a technicality. If you get confused or lost on the day just follow the host of TV crews shouldering their huge cameras who will all be heading for Norfolk's premier fast sport event. When I attended there were crews from the BBC, Anglia TV, Transworld Sports, RTL Germany and at least three other sets of magazine writers and photographers, all jostling for space.

Despite all the media attention it is mainly a children's event, which is the talk of all the local classrooms and playgrounds for weeks beforehand. Congham is in a low lying area with plenty of ponds, so it is excellent snail-hunting country. All the time out of school during the big build-up is spent collecting snails, which are then kept in jealously guarded ice cream boxes and fattened up with a choice diet of cabbage and lettuce leaves to get them into peak sprinting form for the big day. The smaller snails apparently go faster because they do not have to drag such heavy shells along with them.

The course is set on a round table covered with a damp white cloth. Snails move by a series of wavelike muscular contractions and to help themselves they lay down their own track of slime. However, the moist cloth does give them that extra bit of help to avoid sticking to a dry race track.

The course is marked out in two bright red circles. The competing snails are lined up for each heat facing outward from all around the inner circle. The Master of Ceremonies starts each race with a dramatic cry of, "Ready, Steady, Slow!" The snails then have to race for the outer circle, which in a direct line is a distance of exactly thirteen inches, usually helped by shrieking cries of, "Come on Speedy!" "Faster, Cyril!" or, "Run for it, Roger!" as the excitement mounts. The world record holder is apparently a legendary snail named Archie, who once sprinted the course in no less than two minutes, probably helped by the prevailing wind.

Another annual event unique to Norfolk is the Hemsby Herring Festival held on the third Sunday of every August. It commemorates the tradition of Blessing the Herring, which goes back to the times 70 years ago when more than 1,500 fishing boats would be sailing out into the North Sea for the annual autumn herring fishing season. Many of those old fishermen were deeply religious and it was not unusual for the first nets to be cast with ringing cries of, "Over for The Lord". Then, when the first catch was landed, the herring would be blessed with a short prayer for good weather and a good harvest, and for the Good Lord to watch over all those brave souls who sailed out to bring the harvest home.

AT THE HEMSBY
HERRING FESTIVAL,
MEMBERS OF THE
INSHORE RESCUE
SERVICE ARE HARD
AT WORK
BARBECUING THE
HERRING

In those days it must have been almost impossible to imagine that by the year 2000 the last of the huge silver harvests would be finally reaped, the boats almost all scrapped and gone, and most of it only a memory. The herring blessing tradition however, was revived a few years ago as part of a charity fun day which includes a herring barbecue on the beach. The savoury scent of the herring wafts out of the old lifeboat shed on clouds of sweet smoke and steam. Here the herring are to be found sizzling in hot pans, to be served fresh and melting from the bone in hot buttered rolls. It is a feast that would have had those grizzled old herring fishermen of yesteryear nodding their weather-beaten faces in approval.

Norfolk's long sea-faring history is also commemorated in its lavish Maritime Festivals. Great Yarmouth usually gets in first, holding their Maritime Festival in September. The West Norfolk Maritime Festival held at Kings Lynne follows in October.

The long quays at Yarmouth can accommodate a whole fleet of visiting and resident vessels, from small and tall sailing ships to modern cargo ships, sleek naval ships and everything from tugboats to trawlers. One regular visitor is *The Grand Turk*, an accurate replica of an 18th century frigate, three-masted and capable of hoisting twelve working sails. Resplendent in black and gold, even with sails furled she cuts a dashing figure, familiar from her star role in the swashbuckling TV series *Hornblower*.

GREAT YARMOUTH'S SOUTH QUAY, AND SHIPS
ATTENDING FOR THE MARITIME FESTIVAL

Both festivals feature almost non-stop story-telling and shanty singing, and succeed in bringing history vividly to life with full uniform re-enactments, displays and exhibitions. You may encounter pig-tailed seamen, red-coated dragoons, white-wigged merchants, black-patch pirates, or proud young naval officers with golden epaulettes and cocked hats. Or the comic characters like Lofty the Lighthouse and Horatio Herring. Just watch out for the press gangs.

Moving inland in June you will find the Royal Norfolk Show, not only the biggest and best agricultural show in Norfolk, but also one of the major agricultural events in the country. The dominant theme here is to showcase the work and lifestyle of the farming community in particular and the countryside in general, and so the show is woven around the judging of every possible class of livestock. Champions are bred and prize bulls, horses, cows, pigs, goats and sheep all carry off the coveted red, blue and gold rosettes.

At the same time there is a cheerful determination to entertain the public with the most spectacular and colourful attractions in the Grand Ring. The displays can include anything from a freefall parachuting team to the thrilling thunder of hooves and the bouncing big guns of the Royal Horse Artillery. There is always a strong equestrian element with show jumping, parades of heavy horses, and horse and carriage driving.

Finally, as you would expect in a county with both a long coast-line and all the inland waterways of The Broads, there are carnivals and regattas in almost all the major resorts. Sails slice across blue waters, the flags and bunting fly, and boats race up and down. If you have your own boat this is paradise, and if not there is always some waterborne activity to watch and enjoy.

Whether you are a resident here or a visitor, there is much to see and discover, and Norfolk's summer showtime has a whole variety of events to suit all tastes. A visit or a telephone call to any Norfolk Tourist Information Office will tell you what is on, when and where, in any particular area.

TOURIST INFORMATION CENTRES IN NORFOLK

NORWICH
The Forum
Millennium Plain
Norwich NR2 1NF

Telephone: 01603 727927
www.visitnorwich-area.co.uk

GREAT YARMOUTH
Town Hall
Great Yarmouth

Telephone: 01493 846345
www.greatyarmouth.co.uk

KINGS LYNN
The Custom House
Purfleet Quay
Kings Lynn PE30 1HP

Telephone: 0870 225 4827
www.visitwestnorfolk.com

THETFORD
The Ancient House
White Hart Street
Thetford IP24 1AA

Telephone: 01842 752599

CROMER
Prince of Wales Road
Cromer NR27 9HS

Telephone: 0870 225 4853

Other titles from Thorogood

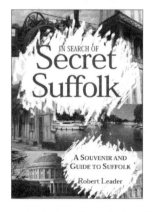

IN SEARCH OF SECRET SUFFOLK

A souvenir and guide

Robert Leader

£8.99 paperback, ISBN 1 85418 209 9
Published 2004

A delightful book of discovery which explores the heritage and subtle landscape of Suffolk. Lavishly illustrated, it follows the course of each of Suffolk's rivers and looks at the towns, villages, stately homes and churches that grew up in their valleys. Robert Leader also charts the medieval history and tradition of the once great abbeys, castles and guildhalls.

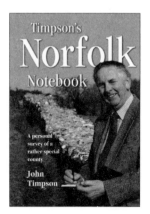

TIMPSON'S NORFOLK NOTEBOOK

A personal survey of a rather special county

John Timpson

£9.99 paperback, ISBN 1 85418 200 3
Published 2002

A collection of writer and broadcaster John Timpson's best writing about Norfolk, its ancient and subtle landscapes, places with strange tales to tell, remarkable and eccentric people and old legends and traditions.

FRONTIER COUNTRY

A walk around the Essex borders

Brian Mooney. Illustrated with maps and pictures by Jon Harris

£8.99 paperback, ISBN 1 85418 214 5
Published June 2004

Journalist Brian Mooney and artist Jon Harris walk all the way round the borders of Essex, exploring the land and people, charms, secrets and surprises of Essex's frontier country. Starting in Waltham Abbey, their walk takes them into old Essex and along the Thames to the marshes and rivers along the eastern seaboard and then back along the Suffolk borders to Hertfordshire. Their account is instructive and amusing and interleaves historical and architectural information with vivid encounters with those who live and work in Essex.

"The authors' unusual journey reveals just how much there is to treasure in Essex"
Simon Jenkins, columnist and former Editor of The Times

BETTY'S WARTIME DIARY 1939-45

Edited by Nicholas Webley

£9.99 paperback, ISBN 1 85418 221 8
Published August 2002

"...a woman who readers will surely love to meet."
This England magazine

The Second World War diary of a Norfolk seamstress. Here, the great events of those years are viewed from the country: privation relieved by poaching, upheaval as thousands of bright young US servicemen 'invade' East Anglia, quiet heroes and small-time rural villains. Funny, touching and unaffectedly vivid.

"Makes unique reading... I am finding it fascinating"
David Croft, co-writer and producer of BBC's hit comedy series 'Dad's Army'

A TASTE OF WARTIME BRITAIN

Edited by Nicholas Webley

£9.99 paperback, ISBN 1 85418 213 7

Published September 2003

A vivid and evocative collection of eye-witness accounts, diaries, reportage and scraps of memory from people who lived through the dark days of World War II. Lavishly illustrated throughout with newspaper pictures and personal photos, the book shows what life was like for millions of ordinary people throughout the war, men, women, children, soldiers, civilians. It brilliantly captures the sights, the smells and sounds and voices of a country at war.

"The wonderful stories… bring all the memories flooding back."

David Croft, OBE, co-writer and co-producer of BBC's 'Dad's Army'

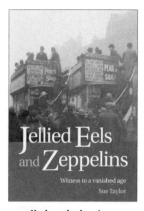

JELLIED EELS AND ZEPPELINS
Witness to a vanished age

Edited by Sue Taylor

£8.99 paperback, ISBN 1 85418 248 X

Published 2003

As every year goes by the number of people able to give a first hand account of day-to-day life in the early part of the last century naturally diminishes. The small but telling detail disappears. Ethel May Elvin was born in 1906; she recalls her father's account of standing sentry at Queen Victoria's funeral, the privations and small pleasures of a working-class Edwardian childhood, growing up through the First World War and surviving the Second. Anyone intrigued by the small events of history, how the majority actually lived day-to-day, will find this a unique and fascinating book.

CONFESSIONS OF A COUNTRY BOY

Keith Skipper

£8.99 paperback, ISBN 1 85418 246 3
Published October 2002

Memories of a Norfolk childhood fifty years ago: this is broadcaster and humorist Keith Skipper in his richest vein, sharp and witty, affectionate and funny. As he says himself "Distance may lend enchantment, but my country childhood has inspired much more than rampant nostalgia. I relish every chance to extol the virtues of a golden age when... life was quieter, slower, simpler..."

"He delights our days and does so much for Norfolk" Malcolm Bradbury

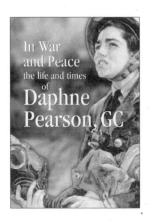

IN WAR AND PEACE – THE LIFE AND TIMES OF DAPHNE PEARSON GC

£17.99 hardback, ISBN 1 85418 211 0
Published 2002

Daphne Pearson, born in 1911, was the first woman to be given the George Cross, awarded for acts of courage in circumstances of extreme danger. This is the inspiring biography of a very courageous and remarkable woman.

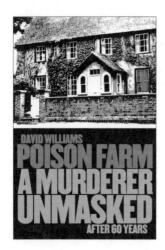

POISON FARM: A MURDER UNMASKED

David Williams

£8.99 paperback, ISBN 1 85418 259 5
Published April 2004

"One of the most amazing murder mysteries ever." Daily Mail

"A classic whodunnit...wealth, sex, scandal and murder in a quiet leafy village." Eastern Daily Press

"Reads like a Miss Marple mystery." Radio Suffolk

A true crime story: investigative journalist David Williams unravels the 60-year old mystery of who murdered wealthy Suffolk business-man and womaniser William Murfitt.